THE UNFINISHED LEADER

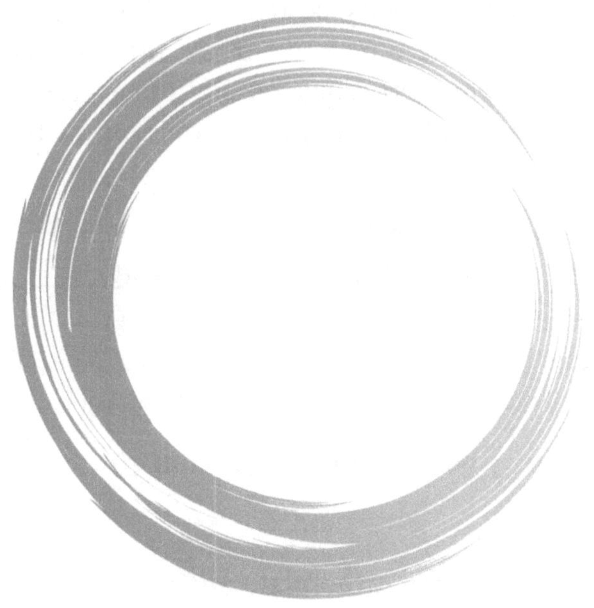

Embracing Personal Transformation
to Lead Change That Lasts

Dr. Laide R. Alexander

Author of *Why Move My Cheese?*

ISBNs: 979-8-9959946-6-4 (special edition)
979-8-9959946-1-9 (mass market hardcover)
979-8-9959946-8-8 (paperback)

For more about Dr. Alexander please visit

www.accexxinsight.com

and

www.thetplat.com

CONTENTS

PART III

THE INNER BATTLES OF AN UNFINISHED LEADER

PART IV

LEADING OTHERS WHILE STILL BECOMING

ACKNOWLEDGMENTS

There is no such thing as a *"self-made"* leader, and there is certainly no such thing as a *"self-made"* book. This book was born out of love, community, patience, and a whole lot of grace.

First, to my children—my first two, who walked with me through nine years of single motherhood, and to all six of you who now fill my life and home with noise, laughter, questions, and shoes in the hallway. You have been my greatest teachers in unfinished leadership. You have seen me tired, overwhelmed, joyful, silly, wrong, and growing. Thank you for loving me not as "Dr. So-and-so," but as Mom.

To my husband, my partner in this wild blended-family adventure: thank you for believing in me when I didn't have energy to believe in myself. Thank you for holding space for my call, my work, my late-night writing, and my early-morning flights. Your love has given me a safe place to be unfinished at home, even while I'm teaching others about leadership.

To my parents and family of origin: thank you for the foundation you gave me—faith, resilience, responsibility, and a fierce work ethic. Being the firstborn in our home shaped me in ways I am still discovering. This book is, in many ways, me finally putting words to that journey.

To the students I have taught as a professor, and to the staff and faculty I have served as a college president and school director: thank you for trusting me with your learning, your livelihoods, your children, your hopes. You have stretched me, challenged me, and proved to me that unfinished leaders can still create real impact.

To the parents and families of our school communities: you put your most precious people—your children—into our hands. I do not take that lightly. Watching the school grow from zero students to thousands has been one of the most humbling experiences of my life. Thank you for walking that journey with me.

To the leaders, pastors, principals, executives, nonprofit directors, nurses, teachers, and community builders I've had the honor to coach and serve: your honesty about your struggles, your questions, and your desire to grow helped me see how universal this "unfinished" journey really is. Pieces of your stories are woven throughout these pages.

To my friends and inner circle—the ones who see me with no makeup, no title, and no stage lights: thank you for reminding me that I am a person first and a leader second. Thank you for the laughter, the prayers, the phone calls, the "Are you resting?" texts, and the gentle confrontations when I try to be superwoman again.

To my *"Why Move My* Cheese" conference community: you are living proof that people can change, organizations can transform, and leaders can grow at any age and stage. You encouraged me, sometimes directly, to put this message in book form. This book is for you and because of you.

To Dr. Debbie McNair, President of Draped in Praise Publishing, who first embarked on this journey with me; to Victoria McNair, whose creativity shaped the initial cover designs; and to Ms. Robin Surface, President of Fideli Publishing Inc., for her invaluable support in bringing this project to completion, and to all my reviewers, mentors, and the behind-the-scenes team who helped shape this manuscript: thank you for pushing me to go deeper, to be clearer, and to be braver. You helped me say what I really wanted to say.

And finally, to God—who has walked with me through every chapter of my story: from firstborn girl to choir member, from divorced mother to professor, from president to founder, from weary to renewed. You have never required me to be finished to be loved or useful. Thank You for trusting an unfinished leader with unfinished people. May this book honor You and serve the ones You love.

INTRODUCTION

The Unfinished Leader

I did not write this book because I have "arrived" as a leader.

I wrote it because I have led for years—in homes, classrooms, churches, colleges, conferences, and communities—while feeling deeply, undeniably unfinished.

If you have ever looked at your life and thought:

"People think I'm stronger than I feel."

"If they knew how unsure I am, would they still follow me?"

"My title sounds more confident than my heart feels."

...then this book is for you.

I have been:

A firstborn child expected to "know better" and "be responsible."

A worship leader leading song with shaky knees.

A divorced woman raising two children alone for nine years— mother, father, provider, protector, preacher, teacher, and nurse.

A professor with students depending on my ability to make complex ideas clear.

A college president tasked with turning around an underperforming institution.

A school director starting from zero students and growing to thousands.

A remarried wife and mother of six, navigating blended family life in real time.

A leadership development expert and conference host, teaching others about transformation while still transforming myself.

Through all those seasons, one truth remained: I am still unfinished.

For a long time, I thought that was a problem. I believed the myth that many of us quietly carried:

A "real" leader is supposed to be certain, polished, always strong, always clear.

By a certain age or title, you should "have it together."

Once people call you "Doctor," "Pastor," "Principal," "Director," "Boss," "Mom," or "Dad," you're supposed to know what you're doing.

But behind closed doors, in honest conversations with leaders across generations—Baby Boomers, Gen X, Millennials, Gen Z, and the emerging Gen Alpha—I kept hearing the same confession, in different words:

"I'm making this up as I go."

"I'm still figuring out who I am."

"I'm not as confident as I look."

"I'm tired of pretending I'm finished."

That's when I realized:

The problem is not that we are unfinished.

The problem is that we are ashamed of being unfinished.

This book is my answer to that shame.

What this Book is About:

This is not a book about becoming a flawless, hyper-efficient, unshakeable superhero leader.

This is a book about:

The art of growth itself—*how real people actually change over time.*

Self-leadership—*how you lead your own mind, will, emotions, and story.*

Honesty—*how you stop performing "finished" and start leading from integrity.*

Courage—*how you keep showing up while still in process.*

Impact—*how your inner growth shapes your family, your workplace, and your community.*

We will talk about the myths that exhaust us:

The myth of the finished leader.

The myth of the all-knowing expert.

The myth of the tireless servant who never needs rest.

The myth that you must fix yourself completely before you can help anyone else.

We will walk through the struggles we rarely admit:

Imposter syndrome—when your title feels too big for your heart.

Over-responsibility and burnout—when "I can handle it" becomes a lie.

Fear of conflict and criticism—when you would rather keep the peace than tell the truth.

Shame around failure—when every mistake feels like a verdict on your worth.

And we will explore the inner life that quietly drives everything:

Your mindset—the stories you tell yourself about who you are.

Your will—what you actually choose, not just what you intend.

Your emotions—the signals on your dashboard you've been taught to ignore.

Your story—the experiences that formed you, from childhood to now.

Who this Book is For:

This book is for leaders in every arena:

In the home: parents, caregivers, older siblings, aunties, uncles, grandparents.

In education: teachers, principals, professors, school founders, staff.

In faith communities: pastors, worship leaders, ministry coordinators, volunteers.

In nonprofit and community work: directors, organizers, advocates.

In healthcare and frontline work: nurses, doctors, managers, chaplains.

In business and government: supervisors, executives, team leads, entrepreneurs.

And for every emerging leader who doesn't yet have a title but feels the pull to step up.

It is also for leaders across generations:

***Baby Boomers**, who may be wondering, "What does growth look like now?"*

***Gen X**: Carrying heavy responsibilities in the middle of life.*

***Millennials**: Navigating burnout, purpose, and authenticity.*

***Gen Z**: Stepping into leadership under the constant gaze of social media.*

***Gen Alpha**: The adults who are shaping them.*

If you are human, responsible for other humans in any capacity, and aware that you are not yet who you want to be—welcome. You are my people.

How this Book is Structured

This book is divided into three parts:

Part I – Breaking the Myth

We'll expose the lies we've believed about leadership and worth, and how they show up in our families, workplaces, and faith communities.

Part II – My Story, Our Patterns

We'll explore how my unfinished journey—from firstborn caretaker to "leadership expert"—reveals the hidden patterns shaping our leadership when we haven't yet faced our own stories.

Part III – The Inner Battles of an Unfinished Leader

We'll walk through my story and yours—our masks, our wounds, our fears, our habits—and explore how to grow from the inside out.

Part IV – Leading Others While Still Becoming

We'll talk about how to create healthier cultures at home and at work, how to develop other leaders, and how to keep growing over a lifetime.

Each chapter will end with:

Reflection questions—to help you locate yourself.

Simple practices—to help you take one step, not thirty.

What I Want for You

When you close this book, I don't want you to feel more pressure. I want you to feel:

Permission to be honest about where you are.

Clarity about how your story has shaped your leadership.

Courage to drop some of the masks you've been carrying.

Hope that growth is still possible in this season of your life.

Conviction that your unfinished journey can bless the people you lead.

You do not have to be finished to be faithful. You do not have to be flawless to be impactful. You do not have to be perfect to be powerful. You are allowed to be in process.

So am I.

Let's walk this out together.

Welcome to The Unfinished Leader.

PART ONE

Breaking the Myth

CHAPTER 1

The Myth of the Finished Leader

If we could gather leaders from every generation into one room—Boomers, Gen X, Millennials, Gen Z, and even a few bewildered Gen Alpha kids—give them snacks, close the doors, and say, "Tell the truth," I suspect we'd hear versions of the same confession:

"I'm making this up as I go."

Of course, that's not what we usually say out loud. Out loud, we say things like:

"I've got it handled."
"We have a plan."
"We're fine."
"It's under control."

We learn early that leadership is a performance. We're supposed to look like we know what we're doing, even when we don't. Where did we learn that? Who told us we had to be "finished" to be taken seriously?

The Performance We Inherited

Think back to the first leaders you watched growing up.

- A parent who always had an answer, even when they were exhausted.

- A teacher who never admitted they were confused, even when the system around them was chaotic.

- A pastor, imam, priest, or community elder who seemed spiritually unshakable.
- A boss who never showed weakness, only results.

Many of us grew up with a silent curriculum:

Leaders don't cry.   *Leaders don't doubt.*

Leaders don't say, "I don't know."   *Leaders don't change their minds.*

Maybe nobody said those words out loud. No one needed to say them aloud. We watched.

- We watched how leaders were praised when they were strong and certain.
- We watched how they were criticized when they wavered or admitted weakness.

So we internalized a rule: To be a leader, you must be *finished.*

Finished products.

Finished identities.

Finished opinions.

Finished stories.

No room for "I'm still learning." No space for "I used to think this, but now I'm rethinking." No category for "I'm growing, and it's messy."

How the Myth Shows Up in Each Generation

The myth of the finished leader doesn't look the same in every age group. It wears different costumes.

Baby Boomers may feel pressure to "stay strong" and never show how tired they are. They think, I've been doing this for 30+ years. I can't suddenly admit I'm still figuring it out.

Gen X leaders often feel squeezed in the middle—caring for parents, raising kids, leading at work. They tell themselves, Everyone is depending on me. I can't afford to fall apart.

Millennials have grown up with comparison on steroids. They scroll past other leaders' highlight reels and think, I should be further along by now. I should already have my life together.

Gen Z is stepping into leadership roles with the internet watching. Every stumble can be recorded, shared, criticized. They think, If I make a mistake, it will live online forever.

Gen Alpha is still young, but they are already being branded, tracked, and evaluated. The pressure to "be something" early is real.

Different generations, same lie:

"If I am unfinished, I am unworthy to lead."

The Cost of Pretending

The performance has a price. When we believe we must be finished to lead, we start pretending, and this pretense always comes at a cost.

It costs us energy. Keeping up an image is exhausting. We're always editing ourselves, hiding certain parts, managing perceptions.

It costs us honesty. We start saying what sounds "strong" instead of what is true. We sugarcoat bad news. We overpromise. We spin.

It costs us connection. People can feel when we're performing. They may admire us, but they don't feel safe with us. They don't bring us their real struggles because we never show ours.

It costs us growth. If we have to act like we're finished, we can't admit what we don't know. We can't ask for help. We can't confess, "I need to grow here." And eventually, it costs us our health.

We burn out.	*We numb out.*
We blow up.	*We shut down.*

Some leaders quit. Some leaders stay, but their soul leaves long before their title does.

A Different Kind of Courage

It takes a different kind of courage to be an unfinished leader. Not the courage to stand on a stage and give a rousing speech. This isn't about the courage to push a new initiative or launch a big campaign. The courage I'm talking about is quieter and deeper:

The courage to say, "I don't know, but I will find out."

The courage to admit, "I was wrong, and I'm learning."

The courage to ask, "Can you help me see what I'm missing?"

The courage to say, "I'm at capacity. I can't carry this alone."

This is not weakness. This is integrity.

It is the courage to let your inner reality and outer presentation match. That's where real growth begins.

REFLECTION: *Where Have You Been Performing "Finished"?*

Take a moment and consider these questions. You don't have to answer all of them now; let one or two resonate with you.

1. In what area of your life do you feel the most pressure to "have it all together"—home, work, faith, or community?

2. What do you fear people would think if they knew how unfinished you actually feel?

3. When was the last time you said, "I don't know," in a leadership setting? What happened—or what prevented you?

4. What did you learn about leadership from the adults you watched growing up? What were you taught (directly or indirectly) about weakness, doubt, or change?

A Simple Practice: Drop One Piece of the Performance

This week, choose one small way to stop performing "finished."
Here are a few ideas:

- *In a meeting, say, "I don't know yet. I'd like us to think about this together."*

- *With a trusted friend or colleague, admit one area where you feel stuck or afraid.*

- *At home, tell your partner or child, "I'm learning how to do this better. I don't have it all figured out."*

It doesn't have to be dramatic. You are not confessing all your secrets to the internet. You are taking one step toward aligning your inner life and outer leadership. This is the first move of an unfinished leader.

A STORY: "I Thought Presidents Were Supposed to Be Sure"

I remember a season when my title said one thing, and my inner life said another.

On paper, I was impressive.

- I was a college president.

- I had the responsibility.

- I had the parking space.

- I had the meetings, the emails, and the late-night decisions that affected real people's lives.

- People introduced me as "Dr. So-and-so" or "President So-and-so," with an air of respect that, if I'm honest, sometimes felt like they were talking about someone else. I would smile, shake hands, and play my part. Inside, however, I wasn't always sure. There were days when I walked into my office, closed the door, and thought: *"I have no idea how I'm going to do this."*

I once faced a particular decision—one I won't detail here because the people involved are real—that deeply impacted students whose lives and futures I cared about but couldn't fully protect. It was complex, political, and emotionally charged, with strong opinions on every side. No matter what I chose, someone would be disappointed, angry, or hurt.

I did my homework. I prayed. I read the reports. I asked for counsel. And still, on the morning the decision was due, I sat at my desk, hands on my forehead, feeling that familiar inner pressure:

"You're the president. You're supposed to be sure."

"Everyone is looking at you."

"You cannot show doubt."

So I did what many leaders do. I put on my "finished" face. I straightened my jacket. I walked into the room and I spoke in a calm, measured voice.

I announced the decision as if it had come down from a place of pure clarity and confidence. From the outside, it was leadership. From the inside, it was performance. The decision itself wasn't wrong; in fact, with time, I still believe it was the most responsible choice we could make.

The problem wasn't the decision itself, but the narrative I believed about what it meant to be a leader while making it. I believed I had to be finished—fully sure, fully composed, without visible struggle—to be worthy of the role.

No one told me that directly, but I had absorbed it from years of watching other leaders, from cultural expectations, from my own story.

Here's what I wish I had known:

That it was okay to say, "This is hard."

That it was okay to say, "I'm holding tension here."

That it was okay to let trusted people see that I was not a machine, but a human being doing my best in a complicated situation.

Being unfinished didn't make me weak.

Pretending to be finished made me lonely.

Why We Cling to the Myth

If the myth of the finished leader costs us so much, why do we cling to it? Because it gives us short-term comfort. It protects us from judgment. If I look strong, maybe no one will see my fear. If I sound certain, maybe no one will question me. It gives us a sense of control. If I act like I know everything, maybe I won't have to face how fragile this really feels. It feeds our ego. Being "the one who has it all together" can feel good—for a while. People come to you for answers. You feel important. But here's the quiet truth:

> *The more we protect ourselves with the performance of being finished,*
> *the more we block the very growth we say we want.*

You cannot expand and protect your image *simultaneously; you have to choose.*

The Hidden Invitation in Feeling Unfinished

Think about a place in your life where you feel most unfinished right now:

Maybe it's your patience with your children.

Maybe it's your courage in hard conversations.

Maybe it's your relationship with money, power, or your own body.

Maybe it's your faith or your sense of purpose.

Most of us experience these places as problems to be fixed.

We say things like:

"I just need to be more confident."

"I just need to stop procrastinating."

"I just need to quit being so sensitive."

"I just need to be more disciplined."

We turn our unfinished places into a harsh to-do list. But what if your unfinishedness is not a defect to hide, but an invitation? What if that place where you feel "behind," "not enough," or "still learning" is exactly where your next stage of leadership is waiting?

The leader who feels like an imposter is being invited into deeper honesty and humility. The leader who is burning out is being invited into boundaries and rest. The leader who avoids conflict is being invited into courage and truth-telling. The leader who hides failures in shame is being invited into learning and resilience. The Unfinished Leader doesn't ignore these invitations. *They listen to them.*

What If You Stopped Trying to Graduate from Yourself?

We talk a lot about "levels" of leadership, "tiers" of development, "next steps" in our careers.

There's nothing wrong with that. Growth is real. Seasons change. Skills deepen.

But somewhere along the way, we started treating our own humanity like a degree we could complete:

"Once I get over this insecurity, then I'll be ready."

"Once I fix these flaws, then I'll be worthy."

"Once I stop feeling fear, then I'll lead boldly."

We are always waiting for a future version of ourselves to start living, loving, and leading fully. What if you stopped trying to graduate from yourself? What if instead you learned to:

Work with your fear instead of waiting for it to disappear.

Lead while still healing, instead of waiting to be "fully healed."

Make decisions while still uncertain, instead of waiting to be 100% sure.

The Unfinished Leader doesn't wait to become some idealized future self to be useful. They show up as they are—awake, honest, committed to growth—and let transformation happen in real time.

Reflection: *Naming Your Myth*

Grab a notebook or the notes app on your phone. Take 5–10 minutes and try this:

Finish this sentence three times:

"A real leader must always ___________."

(Don't write what you think you should believe. Write what you actually feel.)

Then finish this sentence three times:

"I will be ready to lead when I __________."

Look at what you wrote.

Where do you see the myth of the finished leader at work?

Which expectations sound like they came from your family, your culture, your faith background, your workplace?

Circle one sentence that feels especially heavy or true for you. We'll carry it with us into the next chapter.

PRACTICE: Share One Honest Sentence

This week, experiment with one sentence of honesty in a context where you usually perform "finished."

You might say to a colleague:
"This is a stretch for me, but I'm committed to learning."

You might say to your team:
"I don't have all the answers yet, but I want us to think this through together."

You might say to a friend or mentor:
"I'm realizing I've been pretending I'm okay in this area, and I'm not."

You are not dumping your entire inner life on everyone. You are practicing micro-honesty—small, intentional steps out of performance and into integrity.

The myth of the finished leader will not disappear overnight. But every time you choose honesty over image, its power over you weakens. If the myth of the finished leader says, "You must be complete to be credible," then unfinished leadership sounds like bad branding. We worry:

Who will follow a leader who is still learning?

Who will respect a leader who is still healing?

Who will trust a leader who says, "I don't know," out loud?

But look closely at the leaders who have most shaped your life.

Were they impressive, polished, always-right statues? Or were they human? Did they not bleed, doubt, wrestle, pivot, and grow in front of you?

We keep trying to write the final chapter of our story before we let anyone read the middle. Yet most of the transformation people experience around us happens in the middle—in the unfinished parts we're trying so hard to hide. Unfinished leadership is not about glorifying chaos or celebrating irresponsibility. It's about learning to lead honestly from the exact place you are standing, instead of the imaginary place you think you "should" be by now. It's about refusing to outsource your authority to some future version of yourself. It's about saying, "This is where I am. This is what I see. This is what I'm willing to do," and then taking the next faithful step.

The Gap Between Your Title and Your Truth

Most leaders live with a gap. On one side is your title—the role they hired, ordained, elected, or appointed you into. Director. Pastor. Principal. Vice President. Founder. Parent. Supervisor. "The one in charge." On the other side is your truth—how you actually feel inside that role. Unsure. Behind. Stretched. Curious. Anxious. Hopeful. Tired. Awake. For some of us, that gap is small on most days. For others, it feels like a canyon.

You might recognize the gap when:

You're introduced at an event and think: They're describing the LinkedIn version of me, not the real me.

Your calendar is full of meetings where you're expected to "speak into" issues you're secretly still learning about.

People come to you for answers you don't yet have words for.

Your team assumes you're confident because you are decisive, but they don't see the wrestling that happens when the door is closed.

The temptation is to fill that gap with performance: volume, certainty, jargon, busyness, spiritual language, or emotional distance.

Unfinished leaders fill it with something else: truth. Not reckless oversharing. Not "bleeding out" on the people you lead.

Honest truth.

"Here's what I do know."

"Here's what I'm still learning."

"Here's where I need your insight."

"Here's the tension I'm holding."

When your title and your truth are allowed to meet—even a little—you begin to experience alignment. The distance between who you are and who you present shrinks. The energy you were using to "hold the mask in place" becomes available for actual leadership.

That's not weakness. That's power being reclaimed.

The Three Stories Every Unfinished Leader Must Rewrite

Every leader carries stories—quiet scripts that run in the background while we are sending emails, leading meetings, or preaching sermons.

For unfinished leaders, three stories are especially loud:

The Story About Myself

The Story About the People I Lead

The Story About God (or the Bigger Picture)

You don't have to use religious language for that third one. Think of it as the story you tell about meaning, purpose, and what all of this is for. Let's look at each.

1. The Story About Myself

Many of us live with an inner narrator that sounds like a harsh coach or a disappointed parent:

"You should be further along."

"You can't let them see you sweat."

"If they really knew you, they'd walk away."

"You don't get to rest until you prove you belong here."
This story turns your unfinished places into evidence against you.

Instead of seeing your learning edges as normal, you treat them as verdicts: I'm not enough. I'm behind. I'm a fraud. Unfinished leadership requires a new story:

"My growth does not disqualify my leadership."
"I can make mistakes and still be trustworthy."
"I am allowed to be in process and in position at the same time."
"I can lead and learn at once."

You don't rewrite this story in one dramatic moment. You rewrite it in a thousand small choices:

The moment you choose to rest instead of pushing yourself past empty— and you refuse to call that laziness.

The moment you say, "I was wrong," without adding, "but," "however," or a long explanation to save face.

The moment you receive feedback without collapsing into shame or exploding into defensiveness.

Every time you practice these microshifts, you are teaching your nervous system: I can be unfinished and still be safe, still be loved, still be effective.

2. The Story About the People You Lead

The myth of the finished leader doesn't just distort how you see yourself. It distorts how you see your people. If you believe you must be perfect to be respected, you'll unconsciously demand perfection from them. You'll get irritated when they have questions. You'll feel threatened when they bring new ideas. You'll interpret their struggle as rebellion, their slowness as resistance, their fatigue as lack of commitment. Finished leaders say, "What's wrong with them?"

Unfinished leaders learn to ask, "What are they carrying?" and "What do they need from me right now as a leader?" The more you allow yourself to be unfinished, the more room you create for others to be unfinished too. You stop expecting your team, your congregation, your family, or your students to be fully formed, always-on, never-wobbling machines. You start seeing them as human beings in process—exactly like you. That shift changes the way you:

Correct people (from shaming to coaching)

Set goals (from unrealistic to stretching but humane)

Respond to mistakes (from punishment to learning)

Celebrate wins (from "finally" to "look how far we've come")

The story becomes less, "Why aren't you there yet?" and more, "Look at how we're growing together."

3. The Story About God and the Bigger Picture

If your faith tradition told you that "real" spiritual maturity looks like unshakable certainty, flawless behavior, and linear progress, you will be tempted to use God as one more audience you must perform for.

You may find yourself praying as if you are giving a report to a disappointed supervisor instead of talking with a loving Presence who already knows you are unfinished.

You might secretly think:

"If I were truly faithful, I wouldn't be this tired."

"If I really trusted God, I wouldn't feel anxious about this decision."

"If I had more faith, I wouldn't need therapy, medication, or help."

But look at almost any sacred text, any spiritual tradition, and you will find the opposite:

Leaders who wrestled with doubt.

Prophets who ran away.

Saints who struggled with depression, anger, fear, and confusion.

People who led powerfully and still cried out, "Help my unbelief."

What if God is not waiting for you to become a finished leader before you can be useful? What if your unfinishedness is precisely the space where grace, wisdom, and transformation get in? Unfinished leadership trusts that God (or the larger Story you are part of) is not shocked by your humanity. You are not the first leader to feel unsure. You will not be the last.

The Fear Beneath the Performance

If we could strip away the polished sentences and the spiritual language, here is the fear that keeps many of us in performance: *"If people see how unfinished I am, they will leave."*

They will leave my church.

They will leave my organization.

They will leave my team.

They will leave my life.

So we protect ourselves with distance. We project certainty instead of sharing process. We present a strong front instead of confessing, *"This part is hard for me."*

We tell ourselves we are "shielding people from unnecessary worry," when, in truth, we are shielding ourselves from the risk of being truly known. Here's the tension: some people will leave. Some people only know how to relate to leaders who pretend to be gods. Some people are more comfortable with illusions than with truth.

They will misinterpret your honesty as incompetence. They will mistake your humility for weakness. They will prefer the old performance to the new integrity. Still, unfinished leadership is worth it. Because for every person who leaves your life when you become more honest, there are others who will exhale for the first time in years. They will lean in, not away. They will say things like:

"I thought I was the only one."

"I've never heard a leader say that out loud."

"That gave me permission to be honest about where I am too."

Those are the people you can actually build with. Those are the people who will help you carry the weight of leadership instead of just consuming the performance of it.

What Unfinished Leadership Looks Like in Real Time

To make this less abstract, let's imagine a few scenes. You may recognize yourself in one—or in all of them.

Scene 1: The Meeting You're Dreading

You're walking into a meeting where your team expects clarity: "What's our plan?" The truth? You don't know yet. You have pieces of a plan, not a finished blueprint.

The finished leader performance says:

Walk in with a perfectly polished presentation.

Speak with absolute certainty, even if you're not sure.

Shut down dissent so no one sees how shaky the ground is.

The unfinished leader does something different:

"Here's what we know. Here's what we don't know yet. Here are the constraints we're facing. I have some ideas, but I want us to think through this together."

You still offer direction. You don't dump your anxiety on your team. But you invite their wisdom into the process. You model that leadership is not about having all the answers; it's about stewarding the questions well.

Scene 2: The Conflict You've Been Avoiding

There's a conversation you've been putting off—a staff member underperforming, a colleague crossing boundaries, a family member whose behavior is hurting others.

The myth of the finished leader whispers:

"Real leaders handle this without feeling afraid."

"If you were stronger, you wouldn't dread this."

"You're supposed to enjoy hard conversations if you're a real leader."

So you delay, shame yourself, or blow up when you can't hold it in anymore. Unfinished leadership sounds more like:

"I am a leader who finds conflict uncomfortable. That's true. And I am also a leader who is willing to have hard conversations because I care about this person and about our mission."

You acknowledge your fear without letting it drive. You prepare. You pray. You maybe even practice with a mentor or therapist.

Then you sit down, heart racing, and say:

"This is awkward for me, but it matters enough that I'm choosing to have the conversation anyway."

That is unfinished courage. Not the absence of fear. Movement with fear in the room.

Scene 3: The Limit You Can No Longer Ignore

Your body is speaking.

You're waking up already exhausted.

You're getting more irritable.

You're forgetting things.

You are surviving on caffeine, adrenaline, and willpower.

The myth of the finished leader says:

"Push through."

"Everyone is tired."

"You don't get to rest until this season is over."

But if you're honest, this "season" has lasted years.

Unfinished leadership, by contrast, pays attention. It means scheduling a doctor's appointment, talking with a counselor, or having an honest conversation with your board, supervisor, spouse, or team:

"I can't keep leading at this pace. If we want my leadership to be sustainable, we will need to make some changes."

It feels risky. It feels like failure. But it's actually stewardship. Burnout is not a badge of honor; it is a warning light. Unfinished leaders refuse to sacrifice their entire life on the altar of appearing strong.

Practicing Unfinished Leadership in Safe Circles

Not every space deserves your deepest vulnerability. Unfinished leadership is not the same as unfiltered leadership.

Wisdom asks: Where can I be fully honest? With whom? About what?

Think of three concentric circles:

The Inner Circle – a few trusted people (mentor, therapist, spiritual director, spouse, close friend) who see the raw, unedited version of your process.

The Middle Circle – your core team, staff, elders, board, or key partners who see a more processed but still honest version. They hear your questions, your "I'm not sure yet," your learning in progress.

The Outer Circle – the broader community you serve. They don't need every detail of your internal life, but they see enough of your humanity to know you are not performing a role; you are living a calling.

Many leaders reverse this:

They overshare with the outer circle (often online).

They hide from the middle circle (team).

They have no inner circle at all.

To practice unfinished leadership, you might need to build or repair these circles.

Who are the people you can text when you're about to make a hard decision—not for them to fix it, but to hold you in prayer and perspective?

Who has permission to tell you the truth when your performance is getting louder than your integrity?

Who can celebrate not just your wins, but your honest "I don't knows"?

You cannot walk this path alone. Even Jesus had a circle. Why would you be the exception?

Reflection: Where Is Your Leadership Actually Happening?

Take a moment and scan your week—not your "ideal" week, your actual week. Where did your real leadership happen? Where were the moments you had to choose between performance and honesty?

Maybe it was:

The text you sent to a colleague saying, "Can you pray for me before this meeting?"

The decision to tell your team, "We need to slow this down," instead of pushing them past their limit.

The email you rewrote three times until it sounded less like a legal defense and more like a human response.

The moment you told your child, "I'm sorry. I shouldn't have spoken to you that way."

These are not small. These are sacred.

This is where unfinished leadership lives—not just in big vision statements and fiveyear plans, but in the tiny, daily choices to align who you are with how you lead.

PRACTICE: One Honest Adjustment

This week, instead of trying to overhaul your entire leadership style, choose one honest adjustment. Something specific. Concrete. Measurable.

For example: In Communication

"In our next team meeting, I will name one tension we're facing instead of pretending everything is fine."

In Capacity

"I will say no to one additional request that would push me beyond my current limits, and I will not apologize for honoring my capacity."

In Support

"I will schedule one conversation—with a mentor, coach, therapist, or trusted friend—where I talk about the real weight I am carrying in leadership right now."

In Feedback

"I will ask one person I lead, 'What is one thing I could do differently that would help you thrive?' and I will listen without defending myself."

Write your adjustment down. Name when and where it will happen. Then, after you do it, reflect:

What did I feel in my body before, during, and after?

What story tried to stop me? ("A real leader wouldn't...")

What story became a little more believable because I followed through?

You are training yourself to live the truth that you do not have to be finished to be faithful, effective, or called.

You Are Not Behind. You Are Becoming.

If you have read this far and felt exposed, seen, or slightly offended, you are exactly the person this book is for. You might be tempted to turn these pages into another metric:

"Real unfinished leaders do this many honest practices a week."

"If I were really committed, I'd already be over my fear of what people think."

"By now, I should have mastered this."

Please hear this:

You are not behind. You are becoming.

There is no graduation ceremony where you finally receive your "Finished Leader" diploma and never struggle again. There is only the ongoing invitation to:

Tell the truth a little sooner.

Ask for help a little earlier.
Rest a little more courageously.
Admit, "I'm still learning," without apology.

Your unfinishedness is not a liability God overlooked on your résumé. It is part of the way you will lead. Because people do not need one more flawless performance. They need a living, breathing, growing human being who is willing to walk with them imperfectly, honestly, and courageously through the unfinished places of this life.

They need you. Not the airbrushed version.

You.

In process.
In motion.
In the middle of the story.
Still here.
Still saying yes.
Still leading.

Reflection and Practice Notes

The Inner Life of a Leader

If leadership were only about schedules, strategies, and spreadsheets, most of us would be fine. You could take a class, get a template, buy a planner, and call it a day. But you've probably noticed:

You can have a beautiful strategic plan and still be miserable.

You can have the "right" structure and still have a toxic culture.

You can have the title and still feel like a child wearing your parent's shoes.

Why?

Leadership doesn't start with your calendar.

It starts with your inner life. Inside you lies a whole world—thoughts, beliefs, memories, fears, hopes, and habits—quietly running the show while you're busy sending emails. If you've ever heard yourself say:

"I don't know why I reacted like that."

"I promised myself I wouldn't overcommit this time, and here I am again."

"I don't understand why this small thing bothers me so much."

...You've just bumped into your inner life.

The Iceberg You're Leading With

You've probably seen the iceberg metaphor before: 10% above the surface, 90% below.

Let's apply it once more, this time to you. Above the waterline (what people see):

Your job title

Your emails and meetings

Your public decisions

Your social media posts

Your "I'm fine, everything's fine" smile

Below the waterline (what actually drives you):

Your beliefs about yourself ("I'm only valuable if I'm useful.")

Your beliefs about others ("People will leave if I disappoint them.")

Your emotional history (old wounds, unhealed hurts, family patterns)

Your fears (of failure, conflict, being exposed, being ignored)

Your deep desires (to be seen, safe, significant, loved)

Most of us were trained to manage the 10% above the waterline:

Time management

Communication skills

Strategic planning

Performance reviews

Very few of us were taught how to pay attention to the 90% underneath. But here's the uncomfortable truth:

Your inner life is already leading, whether you are paying attention to it or not.

If you don't know what's going on inside, you are not truly "in control."

You are just well-dressed on autopilot.

Mindset: *The Stories You Tell Yourself (Usually Without Noticing)*

"Mindset" is a big word that sometimes gets reduced to motivational posters and coffee mugs. I'm not talking about phrases like "Just think positive!" or "Good vibes only!" If you've ever worked in a real organization—or raised a teenager—you know that "good vibes only" is not a strategy; it's a fantasy. By mindset, I mean the stories you tell yourself about how the world works and who you are in it. For example:

"If I don't do it myself, it won't get done right."

"If I say no, they'll be disappointed and I'll lose my chance."

"If I'm not strong, people will take advantage of me."

"I'm always behind."

"I should be further along by now."

These stories live in the background, like apps running quietly on your phone, draining your battery. You might not say them out loud in a meeting, but they shape how you:

Delegate (or don't)

Rest (or don't)

Set boundaries (or don't)

Ask for help (or don't)

If your mindset says, "Real leaders never need help," you will keep drowning politely.

Will: *What You Actually Choose (Not Just What You Intend)*

Next, let's talk about your will. Not the legal document you sign when you're planning your estate. I mean your capacity to choose—to say yes, to say no, to move toward what matters even when you're tired or afraid. Here's a hard truth:

Your life right now is shaped less by your intentions and more by your actual decisions.

Most leaders have excellent intentions:

"I'm going to be more present with my family."

"I'll stop checking email at 11 p.m."

"I'll finally have that hard conversation."

"I'll make time for my own development, not just everyone else's."

And then:

Another crisis hits.

Another email feels urgent.

Another week disappears.

We think we have a "time management problem." Often, we have a will problem. Our will is busy serving:

Old fears ("If I say no, they'll think I'm not committed.")

Old scripts ("I'm the reliable one; I always come through.")

Old survival strategies ("If I keep everyone happy, I'll be safe.")

Your will is like a powerful engine. If it's wired to the wrong stories, it will drive you in the wrong direction—very efficiently.

Emotions: *The Dashboard Lights of Your Inner Life*

Now the fun part: emotions. Some leaders love talking about feelings. Others would rather attend a three-day meeting about copier toner than sit through one honest conversation about their fear or sadness.

Wherever you fall on that spectrum, here's the reality: Your emotions are not the enemy—they are information.

Think of them as the dashboard lights on your car.

Anger might be telling you, "A boundary has been crossed."

Fear might be saying, "Something feels unsafe or uncertain."

Sadness might be signaling, "You've lost something that mattered."

Joy might be pointing to, "This is aligned with who you are."

If you ignore your dashboard lights long enough, your engine doesn't say, "No worries, I'll just fix myself."

It breaks down. Yet many leaders are driving their lives at 80 miles per hour with:

The check engine light of anxiety blinking,

The low fuel light of exhaustion glowing,

The maintenance required light of grief flashing...

...and they say, "I'll deal with that when things slow down."

Spoiler: *Things rarely slow down on their own.*

The Unfinished Leader doesn't worship their emotions, but they also don't stuff them in the trunk and hope for the best. They learn to:

Name what they're feeling

Ask what it might be pointing to

Respond with wisdom, not just reactivity

STORY: *Your Past Didn't Stay in the Past*

Finally, we need to talk about your story. You did not start leading the day you got your first job title. You started leading the day you started being shaped as a person. Family, culture, faith, race, gender, geography, trauma, opportunity, poverty, privilege—all of these have been forming you for years.

Maybe you grew up in a home where emotions were loud and chaotic, so now you avoid conflict at all costs. Maybe you grew up where emotions were silent and forbidden, so now you struggle to name what you feel. Maybe you learned early, "I'm the responsible one," so now you carry everyone's burdens like it's your job description. Maybe you learned, "If I succeed, I might outgrow my people," so now you quietly sabotage your own growth.

Your past did not stay in the past. It moved into your office. It sits in your meetings. It answers your emails. This is not about blaming your parents or your culture for everything. It's about recognizing that you are not a blank slate with a job title.

You are a story in motion. And if you don't know your story, your story will run your leadership without your consent.

Why This Inner Work Feels "Extra" (and Why It's Not)

At this point, you might be thinking:

"This sounds important, but I don't have time for all this inner work. I have reports due. I have kids. I have a board. I have bills."

I understand. Inner work can feel like something you'll get to "after things calm down," "after this season," "after the next promotion," "after the kids are older," "after the next crisis." But let me gently ask:

How many "after this..." seasons have you already lived through? The truth is, you are already doing inner work. It's just happening accidentally instead of intentionally. You are already:

Making decisions from your mindset

Using your will in service of your old stories

Reacting from unprocessed emotions

Leading out of your unexamined history

The question is not, "Am I doing inner work?"

The question is, "Am I doing it on purpose?"

The Unfinished Leader decides to do it on purpose, not all at once, not perfectly, but deliberately, one layer at a time.

Reflection: Meeting Your Inner Leadership Team

Think of your mindset, will, emotions, and story as your inner leadership team. Today, they might feel more like four coworkers who never talk to each other and keep sending conflicting emails. Take a few minutes to jot down:

Mindset

What is one sentence you often say to yourself when things go wrong?

What is one sentence you say when you succeed?

Will

Where do you keep saying "yes" when you know you should say "no"?

Where have you been putting off a decision you know you need to make?

Emotions

What feeling shows up most for you lately: anger, fear, sadness, joy, shame, numbness?

How do you usually respond when that feeling shows up?

Story

What is one message you learned growing up about leadership, responsibility, or being "good"?

How might that message still be shaping you today? You don't have to analyze all of this right now. Just begin noticing. *Curiosity is the doorway to growth.*

PRACTICE: A 5-Minute Daily Check-In

Here's a simple way to start tending your inner life without adding a three-hour spiritual retreat to your calendar. Once a day—morning, lunch, or before bed—take five minutes and ask yourself:

What am I feeling right now? (Name at least one emotion.)

What story am I telling myself about what's happening?

What do I actually want to choose next? (Not "what do I feel pressured to do," but "what do I want to choose?")

You can jot down one sentence for each. That's it. Five minutes a day won't solve everything, but it will begin building a crucial habit: paying attention to the 90% under the waterline before you crash.

When the Inner Life Refuses to Stay Quiet

Most leaders don't start with a desire to ignore their inner life. They start with a desire to help, to build, to provide, to fix, to serve. They say yes to responsibility because something in them is wired for it. But over time, if the outer demands of leadership keep expanding while the inner life remains untended, the imbalance will surface. ***In your body. In your relationships. In your decisions.***

In the way you talk to yourself when no one is listening. Your inner life will not stay politely in the background *forever. It will knock.* If you don't answer, it will eventually break something to get your attention.

Unfinished leaders don't wait for that break. They listen for the knock.

The Leader Who "Suddenly" Quit

From the outside, it looked like a surprise. A respected department head submitted their resignation on a Tuesday afternoon. No scandal. No angry outburst. No big conflict. Just an email:

"After much thought and prayer, I believe it is time for me to step away from this role."

People were stunned. "But you're so good at this." "We need you." "You just got promoted." They called it "sudden."

It wasn't sudden. Inside, this leader had been wrestling for years:

Waking up at 3 a.m. with anxiety.

Feeling nauseous on Sunday nights.

Dreading Mondays, even though they loved the mission.

Hearing their kids say, "Are you leaving again?"

They had told themselves:

"It's just a busy season."

"Everyone feels this way."

"Once we hire one more person, it will get better."

"Once the budget stabilizes, I'll slow down."

The budget stabilized. They hired more people. The numbness stayed. Their inner life had been trying to speak:

Through fatigue that no vacation could fix.

Through irritation at minor things.

Through a constant tightness in the chest.

They kept overriding it.

"Real leaders push through," they thought. "Other people can quit. I don't get to." By the time they wrote that resignation email, they weren't just leaving a job; they were finally finding belief in their own soul.

The story doesn't end there. Months later, in a quieter role, they said something that stayed with me:

"I thought stepping down meant I had failed as a leader. Now I realize, for the first time, I actually feel like a leader in my own life."

Unfinished leadership is not about clinging to positions at all costs. It's about having the courage to follow truth, even when it leads you away from the version of success other people applaud.

How Unfinished Leaders Relate to Their Inner World

Unfinished leaders are not people who have "figured themselves out" once and for all. They are people who have changed the way they relate to what's happening inside.

Instead of denying it, distracting from it, or disguising it, they begin to:

Name it

Notice it

Negotiate with it

They stop treating their inner life as an enemy to conquer and start relating to it as a source of data, wisdom, and invitation. Here are three shifts that mark this kind of leader.

1. From "What's Wrong with Me?" to "What Is This Showing Me?"

When something in you feels off—tired, angry, jealous, anxious—the instinct is often to attack yourself:

"What's wrong with me?"

"Why am I still struggling with this?"

"I should be over this by now."

Unfinished leaders learn to ask different questions:

"What is this feeling trying to show me?"

"Where have I felt this before?"

"What story is this emotion connected to?"

Anger might be showing you a boundary you've ignored. Jealousy might be showing you a buried desire. Exhaustion might be showing you the cost of living beyond your limits. Anxiety might be showing you a place where you have been carrying a weight alone for too long.

The feeling itself is not the problem. It's a messenger. You don't have to obey it blindly, but you do need to listen.

2. From "I Have to Fix This Alone" to "I Can Bring This into Relationship."

The myth of the "finished" leader dictates that any inner struggles must be resolved privately and swiftly, hidden from public view. Unfinished leaders do something radical, they let other people into the room. Not everyone, but someone:

A therapist or counselor.

A spiritual director.

A wise friend.

A mentor who can handle the truth.

They say sentences like:

"I'm realizing I don't know how to rest."

"I'm noticing a pattern in how I respond to criticism."

"I'm starting to see how my past is shaping how I lead now."

They stop pretending that isolation is strength.

They understand that transformation is almost always relational. Your deepest wounds likely happened in relationship—with parents, siblings, churches, communities, systems. It makes sense that much of your healing will also happen in relationship—with new, safer, more honest connections.

3. From "I Am My Reactions" to "I Have Reactions"

When you've never been taught to observe your inner life, you fuse with it. You don't say, "I am feeling fear." You say, "I am afraid," and then you act as if fear is the whole truth. You don't say, "I notice jealousy." You say, "I'm a jealous person," and then build a case against yourself. Unfinished leaders practice a small but powerful shift:

"Something in me is afraid."

"A part of me is jealous."

"There is a place in me that feels like a child right now."

That language doesn't deny the feeling. It creates space around it. You are more than one emotion. You are more than one reaction. You are a whole person who can notice, name, and then choose how to respond. That space is where wisdom lives.

STORY: The Leader in the Parking Lot

A mid-level leader told me about a moment in a parking lot that changed how she saw herself. She had just left a meeting where a senior executive had given harsh feedback on a project she'd poured her heart into. He wasn't cruel, but he was blunt. "This isn't up to our standard. You need to rethink the whole approach." She nodded, took notes, held it together. As soon as she reached her car, she broke down. She sat in the driver's seat, sobbing. Not misty-eyed. Not one elegant tear. Full-body, shoulders-shaking, "I can't breathe" crying.

Her first instinct was shame:

"This is ridiculous."

"You're too sensitive."

"Grown women don't cry over feedback."

She almost swallowed it. Then something in her—some small, unfinished, honest part—whispered, "Pay attention." She turned the car off. She put her head on the steering wheel. And instead of asking, "What's wrong with me?" she asked, "What is this about?" As she sat there, images came:

Her father criticizing her grades when she brought home a 94 instead of a 100.

A teacher reading her essay out loud as an example of "what not to do."

A college professor laughing at her question in front of the class.

For years, she had told herself those things were "no big deal."

Sitting in the parking lot, she realized her body disagreed. The executive's feedback had not just touched her professional pride. It had ripped open an old wound: "You are not enough. You should be ashamed of trying." She could have driven home, stuffed the feelings down, and let that wound quietly run her leadership for another decade. Instead, she did something different. She called a trusted friend and said, through tears, "I need to tell you what just happened, and I need you to remind me who I am." She scheduled time with a counselor. She began to separate:

"Honest feedback I need to learn from"

from

"Old shame that does not get to define me"

Months later, she told me: "That day in the parking lot didn't make me weaker. It made me more grounded. I still don't like criticism, but I don't disappear when it comes." This is the inner life of an unfinished leader in motion.

Not polished – Not pretty – True.

The Courage to Face What You'd Rather Outrun

There are parts of your inner life you would rather not look at: The resentment you feel toward someone you're supposed to "love." The envy you feel toward someone who got the opportunity you wanted.

The bitterness you carry from a past betrayal. The fear that, if people really knew you, they would walk away. You can lead for a long time without naming these. You can even be "successful." But you will always be building on a fault line. Unfinished leaders are not people who enjoy pain.

They are people who have decided that truth is worth more than image. They understand that whatever they refuse to face will eventually show up sideways:

In sarcasm that cuts.

In decisions that are more about proving something than serving something.

In overreactions that confuse and hurt the people they lead.

Facing your inner life is not about wallowing. It's about reclaiming author-ship. You may not have chosen what happened to you. You do get to choose how you relate to it now. You do get to choose whether it will secretly write your leadership story, or whether you will bring it into the light and write with it, not from it.

PRACTICE: A Gentle Inventory of Your "Unfinished Rooms"

Imagine your inner life as a house. Some rooms are tidy and well-lit. Others are cluttered, dim, or locked. You don't have to fling open every door at once. But you can begin by making a gentle inventory. Take a piece of paper and draw a simple outline of a house. Label a few "rooms" with areas of your inner life:

Fear	Grief
Anger	Desire
Shame	Hope

Then ask yourself:

Which rooms do I visit often?

Which rooms do I avoid?

Which room feels the most "unfinished" right now?

Circle one room. That is not the room you will "fix." It is the room you will begin to visit—with curiosity instead of condemnation. Over the next week, when you notice something connected to that room (for example, a spike of fear, a wave of sadness, a flash of anger), quietly ask:

"What are you trying to tell me?"

"What do you need right now?"

You may be surprised by what you hear. This is how the inner life of an unfinished leader is slowly renovated—not by force, but by repeated, gentle, honest attention.

You Are Allowed to Be in Process and in Position

One of the most paralyzing lies leaders believe is this:

"Once I'm in a position of influence, I lose my right to be in process."

We think:

"Now that people are looking up to me, I have to hide my questions."

"Now that I have this title, I can't admit I'm still working through trauma, insecurity, or confusion."

"I should have handled all of that before I got here."

But life does not wait for your résumé to be complete before it hands you responsibility. Many of you stepped into leadership while:

Still healing from childhood wounds.

Still figuring out who you are.

Still learning how to regulate your emotions.

Still discovering what you actually believe.

If you wait to lead until all of that is "finished," you will never lead. The unfinished leader does not pretend those realities don't exist. They integrate them.

They say:

"Yes, I am still healing, and I am also called."

"Yes, I am still learning, and I am also responsible."

"Yes, I have questions, and I am also committed."

They do not use their unfinishedness as an excuse to be careless. They use it as a reason to be humble, accountable, and honest. The people you lead don't need a leader without inner battles. They need one who knows how to face those battles without pretending, projecting, or making others pay for the wars within. That is the work of the inner life. That is the path of the Unfinished Leader.

PART II

My Story, Our Patterns

CHAPTER 3

Facing My Story:
How I Became an Unfinished Leader

When people see me now—on a stage, with a microphone, speaking confidently about leadership and transformation—they sometimes assume: "She must have always been like this."

They don't see all the versions of me that came before:

The firstborn child carrying adult responsibilities before I could spell "responsibility."

The choir member leading worship with knees knocking.

The divorced woman raising two children alone for nine years.

The college president trying to turn around an underperforming institution.

The school director starting from zero students and believing for more.

The remarried wife and mother of six, leading in a blended family.

The conference host and "leadership expert" who is still asking, "How finished am I, really?"

This is my story. I'm telling it because I want you to see something. I did not become a "leader" the day I got a title. I was being formed long before anyone printed business cards with my name on them. If I don't face my story, my story will still lead me—just from the shadows. The same is true for you.

Firstborn Life: Leadership Before I Asked for It

I am the firstborn. If you're a firstborn too, you probably know this invisible job description well:

Be responsible.

Set the example.

Don't mess up.

Help with the younger ones.

Grow up a little faster than everyone else.

Nobody sat me down and said, "Congratulations, you are now a junior adult." But that's what it felt like. I learned early to:

Swallow my own feelings so that others could have theirs.

Figure things out alone.

Be "the strong one."

Be "the one who knows better."

Though no one explicitly said it, I was being trained as a leader. But I was not being given permission to be unfinished. I internalized a narrative that went something like this:

"My job is to hold things together. I don't get to fall apart. I should already know what to do."

Fast-forward to my adult leadership roles—at work, in church, in my family—and that firstborn script persisted. Even now, when a situation is falling apart, something inside me still stands up and says: "Okay. I'll handle it."

Being firstborn taught me courage and responsibility. It also taught me to hide my need, my fear, and my exhaustion. That is where my "unfinished leader" journey began.

Choir Life: Leading Worship with Shaking Knees

Before anyone called me "Dr." or "President," they called me something else: "You're leading worship this Sunday."

I remember standing in front of the choir, microphone in hand, looking out at the congregation. On the outside, I was the worship leader. On the inside, my thoughts sounded more like:

"Please, God, don't let my voice crack."

"What if I forget the lyrics?"

"What if I start this too high and everyone has to scream the chorus?"

"What if they don't follow me?"

I wanted to lead people into God's presence and not faint in the process. I didn't feel "ready." I didn't feel "finished." I felt like a very visible, very vulnerable work in progress. But I still said yes. That season taught me something that has repeated throughout my life:

Leadership often looks like saying "yes" while you are still in process.

If I had waited to feel completely confident before I led a song, I would probably still be sitting on the back row of the choir.

Nine Years Divorced: Being Everyone for My Children

Then came one of the hardest and holiest chapters of my life: Nine years as a divorced woman, raising my two children alone.

During those years, I was:

The mother and the father.

The protector and the provider.

The teacher, the preacher, the counselor, and the nurse.

The disciplinarian and the comforter.

The one who woke up when they were sick, and the one who went to work in the morning.

There was no "backup adult" coming home at 6 p.m. to share the load. If something needed to be done, I did it. I did not feel like a polished leader. I felt like a tired woman who couldn't afford to collapse. If you had asked me then, "On a scale of 1–10, how finished do you feel as a leader?" I might have laughed, cried, and then asked you to hold this child while I changed that one's clothes. And yet, in those years:

I learned how strong I really was.

I learned how deeply I could love and protect.

I learned how to advocate for my children and for myself.

I learned to keep going when my heart was broken and my body was tired. I was still very unfinished—emotionally, spiritually, financially, and relationally. But I was leading. Those nine years taught me: You can be profoundly unfinished and still be profoundly faithful.

College President: Big Title, Same Human

Eventually, my journey took me into a role that sounded very "finished" on paper: College President. They gave me the title. They gave me the office. They gave me the responsibility of turning around an underperforming college.

People introduced me as "Dr. [My Name], President of [College Name]." It sounded powerful and impressive. Sometimes, it felt like they were introducing someone else. Because inside, I was still:

That firstborn who felt responsible for everything.

That choir member who felt the eyes of the room.

That single mother who knew what it was to have people depending on her.

The stakes were higher now:

Real people's jobs.

Real students' futures.

Real budgets.

Real politics and pressure.

There were days when I closed my office door, put my head in my hands, and thought: "I have no idea how I'm going to do this."

I did my homework. I prayed. I gathered data. I listened. But I also felt the old myth whispering: "You're the president. You're supposed to be sure. You're not allowed to show how unfinished you feel."

The decisions I made in that role mattered, and many of them I still stand by. The problem wasn't the decisions themselves, but the story I carried about what it meant to be a leader: "You must be finished to be worthy of this role." I wish I had known then what I know now:

That it was okay to say, "This is hard."

That it was okay to let trusted people see my wrestling.

That being unfinished didn't disqualify me; pretending to be finished disconnected me.

School Director: From Zero Students to Over 2,000

Then came another wild chapter: Starting a school from the ground up—specifically, the fifth school I had started. Year one:

Zero students.

Zero history.

Zero guarantees.

We had vision, plans, prayers, and a lot of faith. What we did not have were enrolled students... yet. Starting from zero is humbling.

Every new student who walked through the door was a sign of trust:

"We are trusting you with our education and our dream."

"We are trusting you with our safety, our development, and our future."

No pressure, right? As the numbers grew—from 0 to 50, to 100, to 500, to over 2,000—people praised the success. But I want you to hear this clearly: I did not do that as a "finished" leader.

I was still:

Learning how to build systems.

Learning how to manage growth.

Learning how to navigate my own fears of failing all these families.

Learning how to lead teams for that particular project, not just tasks.

I was proud and grateful for the growth. Yet, I never stopped feeling like a student of leadership myself. If I had waited to feel completely ready and fully "together" before taking on the project of starting a new school, those 2,000+ students might not have a story with us today.

Remarried Wife and Mother of Six: Unfinished at Home

Today, my life looks very different from those earlier seasons. I am remarried, a wife again, and now a mother of six:

Six different personalities.

Six different sets of needs and gifts.

Six different growth journeys.

Six different ways to leave shoes in the middle of the house.

My leadership at home is not polished or staged. It is raw, real, and daily. I am still learning how to:

Be present when my mind wants to keep working.

Love each child according to who they are, not who I imagine them to be.

Blend families and histories with tenderness and patience.

Apologize when I get it wrong.

Forgive when I am disappointed.

Rest without feeling guilty.

If you think leadership experts have perfect homes, let me lovingly correct that myth:

No one is more aware of my unfinishedness than the people who see me first thing in the morning and last thing at night.

And that's okay. Home is one of the primary places where my unfinished leadership is still being refined.

Leadership Expert and Conference Host: Still Becoming

Now, I stand on stages, speak at conferences, coach and train leaders, and host my own yearly "Why Move My Cheese" conference. I am known as an expert in leadership development and transformation.

From the outside, it can look like:

"She's arrived."

"She's figured it out."

"She must be finished."

But here I am, writing a book called *The Unfinished Leader,* and I can tell you honestly: I am still becoming.

I am still:

Facing new fears in new seasons.

Letting go of old myths about strength and perfection.

Learning to lead without losing myself.

Learning to rest without losing my edge.

Learning to love my people well while still loving myself.

If someone with my titles, experience, and platform is still unfinished, then you are absolutely allowed to be unfinished too.

What My Story Means for Yours

I've shared my story in detail for one reason: not so you can admire me, but so you can recognize yourself. You have your own versions of these chapters:

Maybe not as a college president, but as a supervisor, principal, pastor, nurse manager, or small business owner.

Maybe not starting a school, but starting a program, a ministry, a department, a family, a dream.

Maybe not a blended family of six, but caring for parents, siblings, or others who rely on you.

Your story has been forming you as a leader. Some parts have given you strength; others have left you with scars. All of it is part of your unfinished journey. The point is not to copy my path. The point is to honor your own.

Reflection: Naming Your Own Leadership Story

I've told you my story in the first person; now I want you to name yours. Open your reflection note page and try this:

Early Life / Childhood

What role did you play in your family? (Firstborn, middle, youngest, only, fixer, invisible one, peacemaker, clown...)

What did you learn about responsibility, emotions, and being "good"?

Emerging Leadership

Where did you first start leading—formally or informally?

When did you say "yes" to something you didn't feel ready for?

Seasons of Pain or Pressure

Divorce, death, job loss, illness, migration, burnout, failure, financial struggle, major change.

How did those seasons shape how you lead and how you see yourself?

Current Season

What roles do you hold now—at home, at work, in your community, in your faith space?

Where do you feel most unfinished today?

You don't have to write a perfect narrative. Bullet points are enough. You are simply beginning to face your story on purpose.

PRACTICE: Share One Piece of Your Story

This week, I invite you to do something brave and simple:

Choose one safe person—a friend, mentor, therapist, coach, spouse—and share one honest piece of your story that connects to your leadership. You might say:

"Being the oldest in my family still affects how I lead today."

"My divorce changed how I see myself as a leader."

"That job where I burned out still makes me afraid to say yes to new things."

You are not required to share everything with everyone. This is not about exposure; it's about honest connection. When you let your story be seen, it loses some of its power to control you in secret. In the next chapter, I'll talk about the masks and roles we wear as leaders—the Achiever, the Fixer, the Rescuer, the Saint—and how my own story pulled me into each of them. We'll keep the same tone: serious about the pain and the myths, honest about the struggle, but with enough humor and hope to remind you:

You can grow. You can change. You can take the next step—unfinished, and still becoming.

CHAPTER 4

The Masks I Wore:
Achiever, Fixer, Rescuer, Saint

If you followed me around through my different seasons, you'd see one woman, many outfits—and I don't just mean clothes. I have worn a lot of leadership masks:

The Achiever

The Fixer

The Rescuer

The Saint

None of these are evil. They all began as ways to cope, to survive, to be useful. But when they become permanent masks, they block real growth.

Let me introduce you to my cast of characters.

The Achiever: "Let Me Prove I Belong Here"

The Achiever in me loves a to-do list. Even better, a to-done list.

As a firstborn, a single mom, a professor, a college president, and a school director, I learned early that results get attention and often bring safety.

Get the grades.

Get the job.

Get the promotion.

Grow the numbers.

Turn around the college.

Grow the school to thousands of students.

On the outside, the Achiever looks like:

"Wow, she's so driven."

"She's always on top of things."

"She never stops."

On the inside, the Achiever whispers:

"If I stop achieving, will I still matter?"

"If I don't overperform, will they realize I'm not enough?"

The Achiever mask helped me survive. It opened doors. It paid bills. It created impact. But it also:

Made it hard to rest.

Made it hard to say "I don't know."

Made it hard to enjoy what I'd already done.

Because as soon as one mountain was climbed, the Achiever pointed to the next one and said, "We're already behind."

The Fixer: "Give Me Your Problems"

As a divorced mom, I had to solve a lot of problems quickly. There was no one else to pass them to.

The kids are sick? Fix it.

The car broke down? Fix it.

The bill is due? Fix it.

Something's wrong at school? Fix it.

Later, as a professor and college president, the Fixer in me walked into rooms full of problems:

Underperforming programs.

Conflicts between staff.

Students in crisis.

Systems that hadn't worked for years.

People would look at me with that silent question in their eyes: "Can you fix this?" The Fixer in me felt important. Necessary. Strong. The problem is, Fixer energy doesn't know how to stop.

So the Fixer:

Takes on other people's responsibilities.

Solves problems no one actually asked them to solve.

Jumps in before others have a chance to step up.

Gets resentful and exhausted, but keeps going.

The unfinished leader in me had to learn: Just because I can fix something doesn't mean I should.

The Rescuer: "I Can Save You"

The Rescuer is a cousin of the Fixer, with more emotion involved. As a professor, I saw students who were struggling—financially, emotionally, academically. Some came from backgrounds that looked a lot like mine; others from situations I could hardly imagine. They would sit in my office, eyes full of worry:

"I don't know how I'm going to pay for next semester."

"My family doesn't support me being here."

"I'm working two jobs and still failing this class."

The Rescuer in me wanted to:

Bend rules.

Take on extra work.

Carry them on my back to the finish line.

As a leader in organizations and in my own school, I've seen staff and team members in crisis. The Rescuer in me has thought: *"Let me just take this on. I can handle it. I'll save you from the consequences."*

Rescuing feels loving. Sometimes, it's needed. But long-term, Rescuer leadership:

Keeps other people from developing their own strength.

Keeps me overextended and secretly bitter.

Confuses being loving with being limitless.

The unfinished leader in me is still learning the difference between support and rescue.

The Saint: "I Must Be the Good One"

Finally, there's the Saint. The Saint wants to be:

Kind.

Selfless.

Sacrificial.

Long-suffering.

Always available.

Always "good."

The Saint doesn't like making people unhappy. The Saint wants everyone to like her. The Saint wants to be the "nice" leader, the gracious one, the spiritual one.

You can imagine what happens when the Saint, the Fixer, and the Rescuer all sit in the same meeting inside my head:

"Say yes, even though you're exhausted."

"Take on more; they need you."

"Don't confront that behavior; you want to be kind."

"Never let them see you struggle; you're supposed to be strong in the Lord."

The Saint mask has deep roots in my faith, my culture, and my story. It has helped me be compassionate and generous. It has also:

Made it hard to set boundaries.

Made it hard to say, "That's not acceptable."

Made it hard to disappoint people, even when it was necessary.

Why These Masks Are So Tempting

Achiever, Fixer, Rescuer, Saint—they all started as survival strategies:

They helped me navigate being a firstborn.

They helped me survive single motherhood.

They helped me succeed as a professor and president.

They helped me grow a school from nothing.

They helped me serve in ministry and community.

The problem is not that we have these parts. The problem is when they become our whole identity. When I forget that I am a person, not just an Achiever. That I am a human, not just a Fixer. That I am a woman with limits, not just a Saint. An unfinished leader doesn't throw these parts away. She learns to see them, name them, and put them in their proper place.

Reflection: Which Masks Do You Wear?

Take a moment and be honest with yourself:

When do you become the Achiever?

When do you slip into Fixer mode?

When do you show up as the Rescuer?

When do you put on the Saint mask?

Ask yourself:

Which mask feels most natural to me?

Which mask gets me the most praise from others?

Which mask leaves me the most drained? You don't have to judge yourself. Just notice.

PRACTICE: One Small Act of Unmasking

This week, choose one mask and experiment with removing it in a small way. If you are always the Achiever, let something be "good enough" instead of perfect. If you are always the Fixer, let someone else handle a problem you know they can handle. If you are always the Rescuer, offer support but don't take over. If you are always the Saint, say a kind but firm "no" to something you cannot do.Notice how it feels.

Uncomfortable?

Scary?

Freeing?

That discomfort is part of your unfinished growth. Masks are not always lies. Sometimes they are the truest thing we know how to offer at the time. They begin as protection:

A way to stay safe in a home that felt unstable.

A way to be noticed in a world that overlooked you.

A way to be "good" in a faith community that praised sacrifice.

A way to survive in systems that were never designed with you in mind.

The danger isn't that you have masks. The danger is when the mask becomes so welded to your skin that you forget there is a person underneath.

When the Achiever forgets how to rest.

When the Fixer forgets how to let others struggle.

When the Rescuer forgets how to trust other people's choices.

When the Saint forgets she is allowed to be human.

Unfinished leadership is not about burning the masks. It is about remembering you are more than any one of them. It is about learning when to set them down.

STORY: When the Achiever Hits the Wall

There was a season when the Achiever in me was winning on paper. Enrollment was up. Projects were ahead of schedule. My name was being mentioned in rooms I had never entered.

The Achiever loved it. Every success felt like confirmation:

"You see? This is how you prove you belong."

"This is how you make sure no one forgets you."

My days started earlier and ended later. 5:00 a.m. emails. Back-to-back meetings. Evening events. Weekend catch-up. One afternoon, I was walking down a hallway between meetings and realized I could not feel my own feet. They were moving—I must have told them to—but my body felt far away, like I was watching myself from across the room. A colleague stopped me. "You okay?" she asked. "Of course," I said. "Just a busy day." It was always a busy day.

That night, I sat at my dining table with my laptop open, half a plate of food untouched beside me, and the house quiet.

I glanced at the clock. It was after 10 p.m. Everyone else was asleep. My eyes burned. My chest felt tight. I told myself, "Just one more email. Just one more report."

The Achiever nodded approvingly. "Good. Keep going. You're almost there."

Almost where? There is always another email. Always another report. Always another metric. I don't remember exactly what broke me that night. Maybe it was the way my hands shook on the keyboard. Maybe it was the realization that I could not remember the last time I laughed from my belly. Maybe it was the voice of God, so gentle and so clear, cutting through the noise:

"If you lose yourself proving you belong, what exactly are you winning?"

I closed the laptop. Not because the work was done. Because I finally believed my body over **my Achiever.** I cried at that table like the world had ended. In a way, it had. The world where my worth depended on my output was cracking. The next day, the emails were still waiting. The reports were still due.

The Achiever in me panicked: "You're falling behind." "People will be disappointed." "You're going to drop the ball." The unfinished leader in me whispered back: "I will not sacrifice my soul on the altar of being impressive." That was not a one-time epiphany. It became a daily decision: to schedule rest on my calendar and keep it like a meeting with my board; to let projects be excellent instead of perfect; and to go home when my body said, "enough," even if my inbox said, "more."

The Achiever still lives in me. But she no longer runs the whole show.

When the Fixer Saves the Day—and Then Loses Herself

Fixers are often celebrated. They are the ones who "get things done. "They walk into chaos and walk out with color-coded solutions. People say:

"We don't know what we'd do without you."

"You always come through."

"You're a lifesaver."

Those words feel good. They also become a trap.

STORY: The Night the Fixer Broke

At one point in my leadership journey, there was a crisis on campus.

A decision from higher up had triggered confusion, anger, and fear.

Students were upset.

Staff were anxious.

Faculty had questions.

The Fixer in me went into overdrive: emergency meetings, drafting statements, calling individuals one by one, mediating between factions, and standing in the gap between headquarters and the campus. For several weeks, my phone never stopped ringing. Every vibration felt like another fire to put out. I was determined: "I will hold this together." One evening, after a particularly intense day, I got a text from a young staff member:

"Thank you for carrying all of this. I don't know how you do it." I stared at the words which were meant as gratitude. I felt a wave of sadness. "I don't know how I do it either," I thought. "And I don't know how long I can keep doing it."

I realized I had quietly agreed to a role that no one had formally given me:

Emotional sponge.

Organizational shock absorber.

Endless problem solver.

In my attempt to hold everything together, I had stopped telling the truth about what was actually mine to hold.

The Fixer in me believed:

"If I don't step in, everything will fall apart."

"If I let others feel the full weight of consequences, I'm being unloving."

The unfinished leader in me had to learn to ask:

"What is mine?"

"What belongs to the system?"

"What belongs to other adults?"

"What belongs to God?"

That meant doing something radical: Letting some balls drop that were never mine to catch. Saying to a team:

"I am here to support you, but I cannot carry this for you. What is your plan?"

Letting a supervisor see my limits: "I can lead this response, but I cannot do it alone. We need more hands or a different timeline." The first time I said those words, my heart pounded.

The Fixer screamed:

"They will think you're weak."

"They will replace you."

Instead, something else happened. People stepped up. Systems were adjusted. Others discovered their own capacity.

And I discovered I was not as indispensable as my ego—and my fear—had led me to believe. That realization hurt. It also set me free.

The Rescuer's Broken Heart

Rescuers often fall in love with potential. They see who someone could be. They see the student who could graduate if only the obstacles would move. They see the staff member who could shine if only they had support. They see the family member who could thrive if only they would choose differently. The Rescuer offers:

Extra time.

Extra grace.

Extra chances.

Sometimes, that investment pays off beautifully. Sometimes, it doesn't.

STORY: The Student I Couldn't Save

There was a student—I'll call her Joy—who came into my office one afternoon with tears in her eyes and transcripts in her hand.

She was bright.

Charismatic: A natural leader.

But her grades were low.

Life had hit her hard:

Working nights.

Caring for siblings.

Financial stress.

A history of trauma she barely had language for. She sat in the chair across from me and said: "Dr. A, I want this. I really do. I just...don't know how to keep up."

The Rescuer in me rose up immediately. "We are going to figure this out," I told her. I rearranged schedules. Connected her with tutors. Advocated for emergency aid. Checked in regularly. There were moments of progress. Then setbacks. Assignments missed. Classes skipped. Stories that didn't quite add up.

I pushed harder. Reminded her of her potential. Extended more grace. Bent more rules. "I can get her through," I told myself. "She just needs someone to believe in her."

One semester, she disappeared. Stopped answering calls. Didn't show up to meetings. Emails bounced back. Weeks later, I got word she had left the program. No goodbye. No explanation. Just gone. I sat in my office with that news and felt two things at once:

Grief for her.

Shame for me.

The Rescuer whispered: "You failed her. If you had tried harder, she would have stayed." But there was another, quieter truth that I had been avoiding:

I had crossed a line from support into over-functioning.

I was working harder for her success than she was.

I was carrying her story like it was my own.

I had confused my role: I was called to walk with her, not walk for her. I was called to offer resources, not rescue her from every consequence.

Unfinished leadership meant grieving what I could not control. It meant facing the fact that:

I am not the Savior.

I am not the Holy Spirit.

I am not the whole answer to anyone's life.

That realization broke my heart. It also released me from a burden that was never mine to bear. I still advocate. I still support. But now I hold this boundary in my spirit:

"I will show up fully. I will not disappear. And I will not carry what belongs to you."

Some students stay. Some don't. Some staff members rise. Some don't. Some loved ones choose healing. Some don't. The Rescuer in me mourns that.

The unfinished leader in me refuses to build my identity on outcomes I cannot control.

When the Saint is Tired of Being Good

The Saint mask is tricky because it looks so noble. It often wears religious language:

"Deny yourself."

"Turn the other cheek."

"Serve without complaining."

"Love covers a multitude of sins."

All of those can be beautiful truths in the right context. In the wrong context, they become weapons you turn on yourself. The Saint version of you might:

Stay in unhealthy dynamics far too long.

Call enabling "grace."

Call silence "peacekeeping."

Call peoplepleasing "servanthood."

STORY: The Day I Stopped Being the "Nice" Leader

There was a staff member who had been undermining decisions for months. Not openly. Quietly. With side conversations. Eye rolls in meetings. Dragging their feet on tasks they didn't like.

Several people had mentioned concerns to me. The Saint in me wanted to believe the best.

"Maybe they're just stressed," I thought.

"Maybe I'm being too sensitive."

"Maybe if I just keep being kind, they'll come around."

So I:

Gave gentle hints.

Dropped subtle comments.

Overcompensated by working harder myself.

The behavior continued. Morale dropped. Other staff started imitating the same passive resistance. I remember one meeting where this person made a cutting remark in front of others. It wasn't overtly disrespectful, but it chipped away at my authority and the culture we were trying to build. I laughed it off in the moment.

The Saint in me smiled. "It's fine," she said. "Don't make a big deal. Be gracious. "Later, alone in my office, I felt a strange mix of anger and sadness. I heard a sentence rise up from a deeper place:

"Your kindness is costing your team."

I realized my "niceness" wasn't just a personal preference. It was becoming a leadership liability. By avoiding a hard conversation in the name of being gracious, I was allowing disrespect to spread. I was protecting my image as the "good" leader instead of protecting the health of the people I led.

The next week, I called the staff member into my office. My heart pounded. Everything in me wanted to soften, to make it small, to apologize for taking up space. Instead, I took a breath and said:

"I need to talk with you about a pattern I've noticed. Your comments and body language in meetings have been undermining our decisions and affecting the team. That's not acceptable here."

They were defensive at first. They denied some things, minimized others. The Saint in me wanted to backpedal. The unfinished leader in me stayed.

"I care about you," I said. "And I also care about this team. If this pattern continues, we will have to talk about whether this is the right place for you."

It was one of the hardest conversations I'd had. It was also one of the most important. Over the following months, the culture shifted. People started bringing concerns to me more openly. Trust increased. Not because I stopped being kind. Because I stopped using kindness as a hiding place. Unfinished leadership means you can be gracious and clear. Compassionate and firm. Loving and boundaries. You are not here to be liked. You are here to be faithful.

The Emotional Cost of Staying in Costume

Wearing these masks for too long has a cost. Not just in your schedule. In your soul. The Achiever runs on anxiety. The Fixer runs on adrenaline. The Rescuer runs on guilt. The Saint runs on shame. Each believes some version of:

"If I stop, I'll be exposed."

"If I rest, I'll be forgotten."

"If I say no, I'll be rejected."

"If I disappoint someone, I'll be unlovable."

You might not say these sentences out loud, but your body believes them. That's why:

Your heart races when you try to decline a request.

Your stomach tightens when you let an email sit unanswered.

You feel a rush of dread when someone is upset with you.

Underneath the mask is a child who, very early, learned: "It is my job to make things okay."

Unfinished leadership does not shame that child. It thanks her. "You kept us alive," you might say to your **Achiever, Fixer, Rescuer, Saint.** "You helped us survive things we should never have had to carry." And then, gently: "But we are not in that house anymore. We are not in that season anymore. You don't have to run the whole show now."

One way to work with these masks is to treat them as parts of you—not the whole you. Set aside ten or fifteen minutes with a journal. Write the name of each mask at the top of a page:

Achiever

Fixer

Rescuer

Saint

Then, for each one, answer these questions:

What do you try to do for me? (Example: "Achiever: I try to keep you safe by making you excellent at everything.")

What are you afraid would happen if you stopped? (Example: "Fixer: I'm afraid everything will fall apart and people will blame you.")

How do you feel when I ignore you? (Example: "Rescuer: I feel frantic, like I have to scream to get you to care.")

What is one thing you wish I understood? (Example: "Saint: I wish you knew I'm trying to protect you from being called selfish.")

It may feel strange at first, like you're talking to yourself. You are. That's the point. You are listening to the different strategies that have been running your life. When you're done, write one response from your deeper, unfinished leader self to each part:

"Thank you for how you've helped me."

"Here is what I need from you now."

For example: Achiever, thank you for helping me reach goals and open doors. I still need your focus and discipline, but I won't let you define my worth anymore. You can help me work hard during work hours, and then you must rest with me.

You are not silencing these parts. You are leading them. This is inner leadership.

STORY: The Day My Daughter Needed a Mother, Not a President

One evening, my daughter came into my room and sat quietly on the edge of the bed. I was answering emails, mind half in another meeting.

"Mom," she said softly, "are you busy?"

The Achiever immediately thought, "Yes. Always."

The Fixer thought, "What's wrong? How do I solve it quickly?"

The Saint thought, "Be sweet. Don't let her see how tired you are."

Something in me—deeper than all of them—said, "Put the laptop down."

I closed it. Turned my full body toward her. "What's going on?" I asked. She hesitated.

"I feel like I don't see you," she said. "You're here, but you're not...here."

Her words landed like a stone in my chest. I could feel defensiveness rising:

"Do you know how hard I'm working for us?" "Do you see what I'm carrying?" But I also heard the truth. She didn't need a list of my responsibilities. She needed my presence. She needed a mother, not a president. Tears came to my eyes. "You're right," I said. "I've been here and not here. I'm sorry. You deserve more of me than that."

We talked long into the night. About school. About friends. About how it feels to share a mother with the world. That conversation did not fix everything But it marked me. I realized how easy it is to hide behind noble roles:

"I'm doing this for my family."

"I'm doing this for my students."

"I'm doing this for the kingdom."

All of that may be true. And still, there are people sitting on the edge of your bed, on the other end of the phone, across the dinner table, thinking:

"You're here, but you're not here." Unfinished leadership means you don't let your masks justify your absence. It means you are willing to disappoint roles in order to be faithful to relationships. That may mean:

Turning down an opportunity that would impress others but cost your health. Leaving some emails unread so you can look your child in the eyes. Saying no to being on one more committee so you can say yes to your own soul.

The Achiever will protest.

The Fixer will worry.

The Rescuer will feel guilty.

The Saint will whisper, "Is this selfish?"

The unfinished leader in you will learn to say: "This is stewardship. This is obedience. This is me refusing to lose myself while trying to save the world."

You Are More Than the Roles You Play

If you stripped away every title, every responsibility, every mask—who would be left?

Not "Dr. So-and-so."

Not "Mom."

Not "Boss."

Not "Pastor."

Just you.

The unfinished, beloved, still-becoming you. That person is not an inconvenience to your leadership. She is the source of it. If you lead from the mask and neglect the person, you will always feel like an imposter, no matter how many people applaud. If you lead from the person and learn to use the mask as a tool—not an identity—you will be able to sustain this for the long haul. You will still work hard. You will still solve problems. You will still care deeply. But you will not confuse your doing with your being. You will not let the Achiever, Fixer, Rescuer, or Saint be the only story. You will remember:

I am allowed to be unfinished.

I am allowed to grow.

I am allowed to change my mind.

I am allowed to rest.

I am allowed to be human and still lead.

The masks you wore helped you survive. Now you are invited to live. And the world does not need another perfect performance. The world needs more leaders who are willing to show up—honest, unfinished, and fully present—without hiding behind the costumes that once kept them safe. That is the work before us. That is the path of the Unfinished Leader.

Reflection and Practice Notes

CHAPTER 5

Teaching While Unfinished: My Life as a Professor

One of the strangest roles for an unfinished leader is professor. On paper, the job description sounds like: "Expert who imparts knowledge to eager students." It's often more like:

"Human beings with a stack of papers to grade, a full life, and a classroom full of eyes waiting to see if you know what you're talking about."

The Weight of Being "The One Who Knows"

When I stepped into the classroom as a professor, I felt the weight of my students' expectations. They came to class with:

Questions.	*Hopes.*
Fears.	*Tuition bills.*

Sometimes, whole families were cheering them on. They were depending on my ability to:

Explain complex ideas clearly.	*Connect theory to real life.*
Prepare them for their careers.	*Give them the tools to succeed.*

No pressure.

Standing at the front of a classroom, I could feel their eyes on me. It wasn't just, "Do you know the material?" It was also:

"Can I trust you?"

"Do you see me?"

"Will you help me get where I need to go?"

I knew, intellectually, that I was qualified. I studied. I had degrees. I'd done the work. But being an unfinished leader means that, even with all of that, part of me still thought:

"What if I don't have enough to give them?"

"What if they ask a question I can't answer?"

"What if I fail them?"

Knowledge, Humanity, and the Myth of the All-Knowing Professor

The myth of the finished leader shows up in the classroom as the myth of the all-knowing professor. You know the script:

Professors do not say, "I don't know."

Professors do not admit they are still learning.

Professors are supposed to have well-formed opinions on everything. If I let that myth drive me, I become a performer instead of a teacher. So, I began to experiment with a different approach:

Saying, "That's a great question. I don't know the full answer yet—let's explore it."

Sharing appropriately about my own learning curve.

Being honest about how my story shaped my perspective.

What happened surprised me. My students didn't lose respect for me. They leaned in. They didn't need a flawless robot at the front of the room. They needed a human guide who was still learning and still curious.

When Students Depend on You—and You Depend on Grace

There were semesters when my life outside the classroom was intense:

Personal grief.

Family transitions.

Leadership responsibilities elsewhere.

Health challenges.

I would walk into class carrying things my students knew nothing about. And yet, they were depending on me. In those seasons, I learned to depend on something beyond my own strength:

Grace.

Preparation.

Healthy boundaries.

The ability to say, "I need help," to colleagues and to God. Teaching while unfinished taught me: You don't have to be perfect to be profoundly impactful.

You must be: **Present. Prepared. Humble. Willing to keep growing.**

Reflection: Where Do People Depend on You?

You may not be a professor, but I guarantee you have people depending on you:

<table>
<tr><td>*Children.*</td><td>*Staff.*</td></tr>
<tr><td>*Clients.*</td><td>*Congregants.*</td></tr>
<tr><td>*Patients.*</td><td>*Students.*</td></tr>
<tr><td>*Neighbors.*</td><td>*Parents.*</td></tr>
</table>

Ask yourself: Where do people depend on my knowledge or wisdom? Where am I tempted to pretend I know more than I do? What might happen if I allowed myself to be honestly "unfinished" there?

PRACTICE: One Honest "I Don't Know"

This week, practice saying one honest "I don't know" in a context where people usually look to you for answers.

Follow it with: "Let's find out." Or "Let me research this and come back to you." Notice how people respond. Notice how you feel. This is not about being unprepared. It's about being truthful, which is the foundation of real trust.

When the Syllabus Meets Real Life

On paper, a syllabus is clean.

Learning objectives.

Reading lists.

Due dates.

Grading rubrics.

It looks so orderly—like learning will move in a straight line from Week 1 to Week 16. But real life does not follow your syllabus.

A student's parent dies. Someone loses housing mid-semester. A quiet student has a panic attack in the middle of class. A global crisis hits and half your students are suddenly caregivers, essential workers, or displaced.

There were semesters when I would stand in front of the whiteboard with my carefully planned lesson and feel the weight of what was actually in the room:

Grief.　　Hunger.　　Anxiety.　　Depression.　　Silent shame.

As an unfinished leader, I had to learn to hold both: The content I was responsible to teach. The human beings I was responsible to see.

Some days, that meant getting through all the material. Other days, it meant closing the textbook, taking a deep breath, and saying, "Let's talk about how you're really doing." That choice never showed up on my performance review. It showed up in emails years later: "I remember the day you stopped the lecture and just let us be honest. I think that's when I decided I could finish school."

Teaching while unfinished means you are always discerning: "What is the most faithful thing to do in this room today?" Not the most impressive. The most faithful.

STORY: The Day I Taught with a Broken Heart

There was a semester when I was walking through deep personal grief. I was grading papers with tears in my eyes at night and standing in front of a classroom in the morning. The two lives felt incompatible:

The professor with the blazer and the slides.
The woman who went home and cried in the shower so no one would
hear.

One morning, I sat in my car in the parking lot and seriously considered turning around and going home. "I cannot do this today," I thought. "I have nothing to give." But the clock kept moving. Class started in ten minutes. My students were walking into the building with their backpacks and their coffee, expecting...me.

I wiped my face. I prayed one of those simple, unfinished prayers: "God, if You don't go in here with me, I can't go." Then I walked in.

I did not tell them all the details of my life. They did not need that. But I also decided not to put on the performance of "everything's fine." I began class differently that day.

"Before we dive in," I said, "I want to acknowledge something. Sometimes we come into this room carrying more than we can see on each other's faces. I'm carrying some things today. I know some of you are too. So if I seem a little quieter than usual, that's why. And I want you to know—it's okay to be human in this classroom."

The room went still. A few students looked at me, then at each other. Then, slowly, they relaxed.

We went on with the lesson. They asked questions. We laughed at a joke. We wrestled with ideas. It was not a magical class where everyone cried and hugged. It was just...real.

Afterward, a student lingered as others filed out. "Dr. A," she said softly, "thank you for saying that. I've been going through some stuff at home, and I thought I was the only one trying to pretend I was okay in here."

She never told me the details. She didn't have to. In that moment, I realized: My job was not to bring a flawless version of myself into the classroom. My job was to bring an honest, prepared, present self into the classroom.

My heart was still broken. My grief did not disappear because I taught. But my students saw something that day:

You can lead and still be in pain.

You can show up and still be unfinished.

The Classroom as a Mirror

Teaching exposes you. You can think you are patient—until the third late assignment from the same student. You can think you are fair—until you realize you're giving certain students more benefit of the doubt than others. You can think you are confident—until a student challenges your viewpoint in front of the class. The classroom is a mirror, reflecting parts of your inner life you might have preferred to ignore.

STORY: The Student Who Triggered My Anger

There was a young man who sat in the back row with his hood up and his arms crossed. Every class.

He rarely took notes. Sometimes he would scroll his phone under the desk, thinking I couldn't see.

When I asked questions, he stared back, expressionless. The teacher in me felt disrespected.

The Achiever in me felt threatened.

The unfinished parts of me, remembering classrooms where I felt invisible, were activated. I found myself thinking:

"If you don't want to be here, why are you in my class?"

"I work too hard for this kind of attitude."

One day, he muttered something under his breath while I was explaining a concept. I felt heat rise in my chest. I wanted to snap. To call him out. To say, "If you think you know more than me, come teach the class."

Instead, I paused. Took a slow breath. And said, "Can you repeat what you just said? I want to make sure I heard you correctly."

He looked startled. He hadn't expected to be invited in. He cleared his throat. "I just said...I don't really see how this applies to real life," he mumbled. There it was. Under the posture and the muttering: a question.

A valid one.

I had a choice. I could focus on the disrespect and make it about behavior. Or I could respond to the question and make it about learning.

"Fair," I said. "That's a good challenge. Let's talk about that. How does this connect—or not connect—to your real-life experience?"

The room shifted. Hands went up. Students who had been silent started offering examples, pushback, stories. We ended up having one of the richest discussions of the semester.

After class, that same student walked up to my desk. *"I didn't mean to be rude,"* he said quietly. *"I've just had teachers who didn't care what we thought. You're...different."*

My anger had not come from nowhere. It had roots—in my story, in my values, in my expectations. Teaching while unfinished meant I had to let the classroom show me:

My impatience.

My ego.

My assumptions about "good students."

And then choose, in real time, how I wanted to respond. Not perfectly. But consciously.

When Students See Your Humanity (and Don't Know What to Do with It)

Not every student wants an unfinished professor. Some are more comfortable with the myth. They want: Clear lines and clean answers. A leader who is always sure and never shaken. When you break that pattern, some will be grateful. Others will be unsettled.

STORY: "You're Not Supposed to Talk Like That"

One semester, I taught a course touching on leadership, ethics, and faith, exploring complex questions—things without easy, one-sentence answers. One day, I shared a story about a leadership decision I later regretted and what I learned from it. I didn't glorify the mistake. I took responsibility. I framed it as growth. Most of the class listened thoughtfully. A few nodded.

Afterward, a student stayed behind, clearly agitated ."Dr. A," she said, "I don't think you should have told us that."

I asked her why.

"Because you're the professor," she said. "You're supposed to be the example. If you admit you messed up like that, how are we supposed to trust your judgment?"

A part of me wanted to defend myself: "I've done far more right than wrong." "You don't know how much I carry." Another part wanted to shrink: "Maybe I said too much." "Maybe I should go back to the safe stories."

Instead, I took a breath and said, "I hear your concern. Can I ask you a question? Would you rather have a professor who pretends they've never made a serious mistake—or one who has, and is willing to talk honestly about what they learned?"

She hesitated. "I mean...both?" she said, half joking. We smiled.

"I get that," I said. "Here's what I believe: you will make real decisions in your life that have real consequences. I would rather equip you with tools for what to do when you realize you got it wrong than pretend that never happens." She didn't fully agree. But she left with something to think about.

Teaching while unfinished will not satisfy everyone's expectations. Some students, staff, or parishioners may prefer their leaders polished and distant. That is not the kind of leader you are becoming. You are not reckless with your story. You are responsible with it. And you trust that truth—even when it unsettles people—is ultimately more loving than illusion.

The Student Who Taught Me About Dignity

One of the greatest gifts of teaching while unfinished is realizing that learning is not one-directional. You are not the only one bringing wisdom into the room. Your students are image-bearers with their own experiences, insight, and resilience. They will teach you—if you let them.

STORY: "Please Don't Pity Me"

There was a student who often fell asleep in class, head down on the desk, eyes fluttering. I would wake her gently. She would apologize, clearly embarrassed. My first instinct was to interpret it as disrespect or lack of discipline. But something in her face made me pause.

After class one day, I asked, "Can you stay for a minute?" She stayed, shoulders tense. "I want you to know," I said, "I'm not angry with you. But I've noticed you've been really tired in class lately. Is there something going on that I should know about?"

She stared at the floor for a long time. Finally, she said, "I'm working full-time nights at the hospital. I get off at 7 a.m., go home to get my little brothers ready for school, then come straight here. I try to stay awake. I really do."

My heart broke.

"Why didn't you tell me?" I asked softly. She shrugged. "I didn't want you to think I was making excuses. And I didn't want you to...pity me." That sentence landed heavy: "I didn't want you to pity me."

In that moment, I realized how easy it is, even with good intentions, to treat struggling students as charity cases instead of as dignified adults navigating impossible choices. I had to examine my own heart: Was I willing to see her as a capable, resilient woman making heroic efforts—not just a "tired student"? Was I willing to adjust my expectations without lowering my respect?

We talked about options: Adjusting deadlines when possible. Finding campus resources. Strategies to manage her energy. But what she needed most was not a new policy. She needed to know: "I see you. I respect you. I'm not lowering the bar because I think you can't do it. I'm going to work with you because I believe you can."

Teaching while unfinished meant admitting to myself how quickly I had almost written her off as "unmotivated." She changed the way I looked at every sleeping student after that. Instead of annoyance, I learned to ask: "What might be happening in their life that I cannot see?" Not to excuse everything. But to humanize everything.

When You Don't Have the Energy to Care as Much as You Used To

There is a particular pain that comes when you realize your compassion is thinning. You remember the version of yourself who knew every student's story. Stayed after class to listen. Went the extra mile again and again.

And now, you're tired. You close your office door more often. You feel irritated by needs that used to move you.

You might wonder: "Have I become hard?" "Am I burned out?" "Should I even be doing this anymore?"

Teaching while unfinished means being honest about compassion fatigue.

STORY: The Semester I Started to Numb Out

There was a stretch where every advisee who walked into my office seemed to be in crisis. One had just left an abusive relationship. Another was facing deportation. Another was battling suicidal thoughts. I cared deeply. I also felt like I was drowning. I found myself dreading student appointments. Not because I didn't love them. But because I feared what new pain I would have to hold.

One afternoon, a student sat across from me, telling me about a family situation so painful that months earlier, I would have been in tears with her. That day, I felt...nothing. I nodded. I gave appropriate responses. I offered resources. But inside, I was numb. After she left, I sat there, disturbed. "When did I stop feeling?" I wondered. "What did I do with all that pain?"

I hadn't been irresponsible. I had been overloaded. My empathy circuit had gone into self-protection mode. Teaching while unfinished meant I had to face that—not hide it. I reached out to a therapist. I had hard conversations with myself about workload, boundaries, and the Savior complex that had me believing I had to hold everything for everyone.

I talked with a trusted colleague and said, "I'm worried that I'm starting to shut down. I don't want to become that kind of professor." We made a plan: Sharing some of the emotional load. Creating referral pathways so I wasn't the only "safe adult" for every hurting student. Building in time to decompress after heavy conversations.

My feeling gradually returned. Not all at once. But enough. Enough to remind me that my numbness had not been a moral failure. It had been a warning sign. Unfinished leaders pay attention to those signs—not to indulge themselves, but to protect the integrity of their care.

The Quiet Students Who Are Watching

Not every student will speak in class. Some will never raise their hand. They sit on the edges, taking everything in. They may never email you. They may never come to office hours. You may assume they are disengaged. Years later, they will write to you and say something like:

"You don't remember me, but I sat in the back row of your 8 a.m. class. I never talked. But I watched how you treated people. It changed the way I saw myself."

Teaching while unfinished means accepting that your impact is not always visible. You may never see the full harvest of the seeds you plant. But they are there. The way you:

Respond to a wrong answer.

Handle a disrespectful comment.

Talk about people who are different from you.

Admit your own mistakes.

All of that is curriculum.

Your character is part of the course.

You are teaching, even when you're not "teaching.

PRACTICE: A "Whole Room" Scan

Before your next meeting, class, or gathering where people look to you for guidance, try this: Arrive two minutes early if you can. Sit or stand where you can see the room.

Do a silent scan. Not to judge, but to notice:

Who looks tired?

Who looks anxious?

Who looks shut down?

Who looks eager?

Ask quietly: "What might this room need from me today—not just intellectually, but emotionally and spiritually?" Set one intention. It could be:

"I will slow down and make space for questions."

"I will affirm one quiet student."

"I will name the difficulty of what we're carrying this week."

Then teach.
Lead.
Guide.
Not perfectly.
Presently.

Afterward, take sixty seconds to reflect:

"What did I notice?"

"How did my presence feel different when I paid attention to the whole room, not just my notes?"

This is unfinished leadership in action. Not a new technique. A new way of being in the same space.

You Don't Have to Be the Final Word to Be a Faithful Teacher

As a professor, it's tempting to believe you must give students "the answer." The definitive perspective. The last word. Unfinished leadership holds that role differently.

You are not the final word.

You are a voice.

A guide.

A witness.

You are one person in the long line of people who will shape your students' minds and hearts. You will not fix everything that was broken before they arrived. You will not prevent every hurt they will experience after they leave. But you can: Model what it looks like to think critically and compassionately. Show them how to admit, "I was wrong," without collapsing.

Demonstrate how to hold faith and doubt in the same hand. Teach them that authority and humility can live in the same body. You can be a living example of an unfinished leader:

Still reading.

Still listening.

Still repenting.

Still growing.

And maybe, years from now, when they are in positions of influence—classrooms, boardrooms, pulpits, clinics, kitchens—they will remember:

"I had a professor who didn't pretend to know everything, but she knew how to keep learning. I can do that too."

That is legacy. Not a perfect professor.

An honest one.

An unfinished one.

Still showing up.

Still teaching.

Still becoming.

The Inner Battles
of an Unfinished Leader

Imposter Syndrome: When Your Title Feels Too Big

I have held titles that felt heavier than the nameplate on my door:

President	Founder	Professor
Expert	"Woman of God"	"Strong leader"

And many times, inside, I have felt like I was still that first-born girl, that nervous choir member, that tired single mom, thinking: "Are you sure they meant me?"

The Secret Questions Behind the Strong Face

Imposter syndrome is not always loud. Sometimes, it's a quiet background noise. For me, it has sounded like:

"If they really knew how unsure I feel, would they still listen to me?"

"If they saw my fears, my bad day, my doubts, would they still call me a leader?"

"Did I just get lucky? Am I one mistake away from being exposed?"

The more visible my roles became, the louder these questions tried to be. That's the strange math of imposter syndrome: The higher you rise, the more your fear insists you don't belong.

Where Imposter Syndrome Meets My Story

Imposter syndrome doesn't come from nowhere. It connects to our stories. In my case:

As a firstborn, I learned to carry more than my age.

As a divorced woman, I knew what it was to feel judged.

As a Black woman, I have navigated spaces where I had to work twice as hard to be seen as competent.

As a woman in leadership, I have entered rooms where my presence was questioned before I even opened my mouth. All of this feeds the inner voice that says: *"You must prove you belong here. And even then, it might not be enough."*

Telling the Truth About Imposter Feelings

Here's what I've learned: *Feeling like an imposter does not mean you are one.* It means:

You are aware of the gap between your ideal and your reality.

You are stepping into spaces that stretch you.

You care deeply about doing things well.

Imposter syndrome becomes dangerous when it makes you shrink (you stop applying, stop speaking, stop risking). Or it makes you perform (you overcompensate, overwork, overprove).

An unfinished leader learns to name imposter feelings without obeying them.

Reflection: Where Do You Feel Like a Fraud? Ask yourself:

In which role do I most often feel like a fraud—parent, partner, pastor, boss, expert, friend?

What is the story behind that feeling? (Family expectations, past mistakes, cultural messages, etc.)

Who benefits if I keep believing I don't belong here? *Hint:* It is not you. And it is not the people you're called to serve.

PRACTICE: A New Inner Script

This week, when you notice imposter thoughts, try responding with a new script:

"I feel like an imposter right now, and I am still showing up."

"I don't know everything, but I know enough to be useful here."

"Growth feels like this—stretchy and uncertain."

You are not lying to yourself. You are telling a fuller truth.

Imposter syndrome is so common and so deeply felt that it deserves more than a definition. It deserves a witness. You are not the only one who has walked into a room, sat at a table, opened a Zoom call, or stood behind a podium and thought: "Any minute now, they're going to realize they picked the wrong person." You are not the only one who has scrolled past your own bio and thought, "That sounds like someone else."

You are not the only one who has prayed, "God, are You sure? Me?" This "syndrome" is not an abstract concept. It is lived, daily, in the bodies and stories of unfinished leaders.

The Hidden Exhaustion of Pretending You're Sure

Imposter syndrome doesn't always look like insecurity on the outside. Sometimes it looks like:

Overpreparing for everything.

Never turning your phone off.

Saying yes to every invitation.

Staying three steps ahead so you're never caught offguard. People praise you for your excellence, your responsiveness, your reliability. They have no idea how much of it is fueled by fear.

Fear of being "found out."

Fear of being replaced.

Fear of confirming someone's stereotype about you. You might be the one others call "confident," "strong," "steady." They don't see the rituals you go through before you show up:

Rewriting your email five times so you don't sound "too emotional" or "too ignorant."

Practicing your introduction in the mirror so you don't stumble over your own title.

You check your notes over and over, determined no one will say you weren't prepared. Your performance is polished, but your inner life is often frantic.

Unfinished leadership begins when you tell the truth about that gap—not just to God, but to yourself.

STORY: The President in the Parking Lot

There was a morning, early in my presidency, when I sat in my car in the parking lot, hands on the steering wheel, unable to move. I had a full day ahead: A budget meeting. A faculty forum. A call with headquarters. Student concerns waiting in my inbox. I had prepared.

I knew the agenda. I knew the talking points. And yet, sitting in that car, all I could think was: *"They think a president is walking into that building. What if they get me instead?"* I imagined the faces around the board table, the expectations in their eyes. I imagined the faculty who had been at the institution longer than I had, measuring my decisions against decades of history. I imagined students who had pinned their hopes on this place, on me. The imposter voice hissed:

"You're the experiment."

"You're the diversity hire."

"You're here until they find someone 'more qualified.'"

I could feel my heart pounding. My palms were sweaty on the steering wheel. For a moment, I thought, "What if I just…drive away?"

Not forever.

Just for today.

Just long enough to avoid being seen.

Then another voice—quieter, but steadier—rose up:

"You have walked through too much to let a parking lot stop you. You did not put yourself here. You have work to do."

I sat there and cried—mascara, title, and all. Then I wiped my face, took a deep breath, and said out loud, to no one and to God:

"I feel like an imposter today. But I am still going to walk in there and lead."

I did.

It was not a perfect day. I missed something in the budget meeting. I stumbled over an answer in the forum. I had to say, "I don't know yet," more than once. No one fired me. No one stood up and shouted, "Fraud!" People asked good questions, gave feedback, and disagreed respectfully. The building did not fall. What cracked that day was not my credibility. It was the illusion that I had to feel like a president to be one. Sometimes, you have to act from your calling while your emotions catch up. *That is not deception. That is courage.*

Imposter Syndrome Wears Different Faces

Imposter syndrome doesn't sound the same in every leader. It shapeshifts, depending on your story.

For the FirstGeneration Leader

Maybe you're the first in your family to:

Go to college.

Start a business.

Lead a ministry.

Earn a doctorate.

Your people are proud of you.

They also don't fully understand what you do. You straddle two worlds:

The world you came from.

The world you're now leading in.

In one world, you feel **"too much."**

Too educated.

Too ambitious.

Too "different."

In the other, you feel **"not enough."**

Not polished enough.

Not connected enough.

Not "from the right background."

Every time you walk into a room with people who have legacies and last names that open doors, you may hear: *"You're just pretending to belong here. Don't forget where you came from."* Honoring your roots and owning your rise are not mutually exclusive. You are not betraying your people by growing. You are expanding what is possible for them.

For the Leader from a Marginalized Identity

If you are a woman, a person of color, an immigrant, differentlyabled, or hold any identity that has historically been pushed to the edges, imposter syndrome is not just internal. It is reinforced by:

Being the only one like you in the room.

Hearing, "You're so articulate," as if that's a surprise.

Being mistaken for support staff when you're the keynote speaker.

Having your expertise questioned in ways your peers don't experience. You are not imagining that. The system is real. You have receipts. So when you hear that inner voice say, *"You don't belong here,"* it is layered with the actual experiences of being treated like you don't. Unfinished leadership doesn't ask you to gaslight yourself. It invites you to hold both:

"Yes, the environment is biased and often unfair."

"And still, I am here on purpose, not by accident. My presence is not a favor. It is a contribution."

For the "Always Strong One"

Maybe your imposter feelings don't show up as *"I don't belong."* They show up as: *"If I'm ever not strong, people will see I'm not who they think I am."* You have built a life around being the reliable one. The one people lean on. The one who *"never breaks."* So even when you're exhausted, you keep smiling. Even when you're grieving, you keep leading. You think:

"If they see my weakness, they'll lose faith in me."

"If I ask for help, they'll think I've been faking this whole time."

The truth? The longer you pretend, the more you are faking. Not your competence. Your humanity.

Unfinished leaders discover that the most trustworthy strength is not the one that never bends. It is the one that can say, *"I am tired,"* and *still be faithful.*

STORY: The Panel I Almost Talked Myself Out Of

There was a conference where I'd been invited to sit on a panel with leaders I admired. Their bios read like a highlight reel:

Books.

Awards.

National platforms.

Mine...did not. The night before, I lay in my hotel bed staring at the ceiling, listing reasons I did not belong:

"They've been in this field longer than you."

"They've built bigger things than you."

"They sound smarter than you."

I thought about emailing the organizer: "I'm sick. I can't make it."

Was it entirely untrue? My stomach did hurt. My chest was tight. My voice did feel shaky. But I knew that wasn't illness.

That was fear.

Lying there in the dark, I asked myself a hard question:

"Who does it serve if you stay home?"

It wouldn't serve the audience, who would get one less perspective.

It wouldn't serve the organizer, who invited you for a reason.

It wouldn't serve your younger self, who prayed for a day like this.

It would only serve your fear.

The next day, I sat on that stage, hands resting in my lap to hide the trembling. The first few questions went to the "bigger names." Then the moderator turned to me. *"Dr. Alexander, what's your take on this?"*

For a split second, my mind went blank. Then I remembered:

My story.

My students.

The people I had led and loved.

I answered from there. Not from trying to sound like anyone else. Not from trying to impress, but from my lived experience.

Afterward, several people came up to me and said:

"When you talked about leading while still healing, that's what I needed."

"Your story sounded like mine."

No one said, *"You didn't belong up there."*

No one said, *"We were hoping for someone else."*

The only person judging me so harshly was myself.

When Competence and Confidence Don't Arrive Together

We often assume that competence and confidence arrive as a package deal:

Once I'm competent, I'll feel confident.

Once I know enough, I'll stop doubting.

But many of the most competent leaders I know still battle imposter feelings. Why?

Because competence is about what you can do.

Confidence is about what you believe about what you can do.

You can have a long track record of:

Making sound decisions,

Building healthy teams,

Navigating crises,

...and still feel like you're "faking it." Imposter syndrome is not solved by more achievements. If it were, your degrees, titles, and accomplishments would have cured it by now. What begins to heal it is:

Telling the truth about your fear. Updating the story you tell yourself about what qualifies you. Anchoring your identity in something deeper than your performance. Unfinished leaders understand:

"I may not always feel like I belong in this room, but my feelings are not the final authority on my calling."

The Cost of Letting Imposter Syndrome Lead

Imposter syndrome is not just an internal experience. It has external consequences. When you believe you're a fraud, you will unconsciously:

Overcompensate.

You overwork to earn a place you already have, burning yourself out.

Under-risk.

You avoid new opportunities, fearing they'll expose you, so you stay safely inside what you've already mastered.

Over-edit.

You water down your voice, trying not to offend, not to stand out, not to be "too much."

Under-delegate.

You hoard tasks because, "If someone else can do this, maybe I'm not that special after all."

The people you lead pay for this. They get a leader who is:

Tired.

Hesitant.

Controlling.

Less creative.

Not because you don't love them. Because you are busy fighting ghosts. Unfinished leadership means you start asking:

"What would I do differently if I believed, fully, that I belonged here?"

"What opportunities am I saying no to—not because they're unwise, but because I'm afraid?"

"Who is God trying to bless through my presence that I keep hiding?"

STORY: The Promotion I Tried to Decline

Before I became a president, I was offered a leadership promotion in another context. On paper, it was a clear next step. The people around me were excited. "This makes sense," they said. "You've been doing the work already." Inside, I panicked. I saw every area where I was still learning. Every gap in my knowledge. Every weakness that might be magnified. I sat in my supervisor's office and said, *"I'm not sure I'm the right person. "*He leaned back in his chair and asked, *"Why?"*

I listed my reasons:

"I've never led at that level before. "

"There are people with more experience than me. "

"I'm still figuring out my leadership style. "

He listened quietly. Then he said, *"Laide, we are not promoting you because you have no growth left. We're promoting you because of how you handle your growth. "*

That sentence stayed with me. They weren't looking for a finished leader. They were looking for an unfinished one who was honest, teachable, and courageous. I accepted the role. Not because my imposter feelings disappeared. Because I decided they would not make the decision for me.

Naming the Lies That Feed Imposter Syndrome

Imposter syndrome feeds on unexamined beliefs. Here are a few common ones:

"A real leader always knows what to do."

"If I make a big mistake, it means I should never have been in this role."

"If I ask for help, people will realize I'm not as capable as they thought."

"If I don't have the same background as others here, I must be less qualified."

"If I feel afraid, it means I'm not called."

Unfinished leaders drag these beliefs into the light and interrogate them. Try writing them down and asking:

"Where did I learn this?"

"Is it actually true?"

"Who am I trying to protect by believing this?"

"What does my story—and God's story—say instead?"

For example:

Lie: "If I don't know everything, I shouldn't be here."

Truer story: "No one knows everything. My willingness to learn and listen is part of why I'm here."

Lie: "If I make a mistake, I'll prove everyone right who doubted me."

Truer story: "My mistakes will show how I repair, not whether I'm worthy to exist."

This is not positive thinking. It is retraining your inner narrator to tell the truth.

PRACTICE: A "Receipts" List

Imposter syndrome says, "You have no business being here."

Facts say otherwise. This week, set aside ten minutes to make a "Receipts List." Divide a page into three columns:

Role (e.g., teacher, manager, parent, pastor, entrepreneur)

Evidence of Faithfulness (not perfection—faithfulness)

What This Says About Me

For example:

Role: Team Leader

Evidence: Led my team through a difficult reorganization without losing anyone.

What This Says: I can navigate change with care and clarity.

Role: Parent

Evidence: My child came to me with a hard truth instead of hiding it.

What This Says: I am building enough safety for honesty.

Role: Speaker

Evidence: After my talk, two people shared how it helped them make a decision.

What This Says: My words can be useful, even when I feel nervous.

Keep this list somewhere you can see it—not to boast, but to counteract the amnesia that imposter syndrome creates. When the voice says, "You've never done anything that proves you belong," you can gently respond: *"That's not true. I have receipts."*

STORY: When a Student Called Me "Dr. A" for the First Time

Imposter syndrome doesn't just show up in high-profile moments. It shows up in the tiny, everyday ones. The first time a student called me "Dr. A," I looked over my shoulder to see who they were talking to. It hit me in waves:

The little girl who used to speak into her grandmother's standing fan (using it as a microphone) pretends to be speaking to a sea of people.

The teenager who was told, **"You're too much."**

The single mom who did homework after putting the kids to bed.

The woman who defended her dissertation, heart pounding, wondering if it was "enough."

All of them were in that moment. The imposter voice whispered:

"It's just a title."

"Don't get used to it."

Another voice, deeper, more rooted, said:

"You did not steal this. You earned it. You received it. You steward it."

I didn't correct the student. I didn't wave it off. I said, "Yes? "Sometimes, healing imposter syndrome starts with letting yourself answer to the name you've already been given.

Not shrinking.

Not apologizing.

Not over-explaining.

Just...owning it.

You Are Not the Mistake in the Room

Imposter syndrome convinces you that you are the exception:

Everyone else is supposed to be here. You are the accident.

Everyone else is qualified. You are the oversight.

Everyone else is "real." You are the stand-in until they find someone better.

If you could see what other leaders think in their quiet moments, you would discover: ***You are not the only one.***

The executive who intimidates you lies awake at night wondering if she's in over her head. The pastor whose sermons move you wonders if he's said anything new in years. The professor whose work you cite rereads their own writing and cringes at old sentences. We are all, in different ways, leading while unfinished. The difference is not who feels like an imposter. The difference is who lets that feeling define their obedience.

Unfinished leaders feel the fear, hear the questions, notice the tremor in their voice—and still stand up, still speak, still decide, still love. Not because they are sure they are **"enough."** But, Because they are sure that hiding is no longer an option.

You may never silence the imposter voice completely. But you can turn down its volume. You can stop giving it the final vote. You can let your calling, your community, your character, and your God speak louder than your fear. And over time, you may notice something gentle and radical happening:

The title that once felt too big starts to feel...true.

Not because you became perfect.

Because you stayed.

You kept showing up.

You led, not as a finished product, but as an unfinished leader—honest, growing, human, and still here.

CHAPTER 7

Burnout, Over-Responsibility, and the Lie of "I Can Handle It"

If there were frequent flyer miles for burnout, I'd have status.

I have lived in the neighborhood of over-responsibility:

As a firstborn.

As a single mother.

As a professor with students depending on me.

As a college president with an institution depending on me.

As a founder with families and organizations depending on me.

As a wife and mother of six with a whole household depending on me.

My default sentence used to be: "It's okay. I can handle it."

Spoiler: I could not always handle it. But I tried.

When Caring Turns Into Carrying

There is a difference between caring for people and carrying people. Caring looks like:

Support.	Guidance.
Healthy sacrifice.	Clear limits.

Carrying looks like: Taking on what isn't yours. Saying yes when you're already at capacity. Doing other's emotional, spiritual, or practical work for them, or collapsing later, often in private.

I crossed that line many times. Saying yes to every extra request. Solving problems others could have solved. Being the emotional support, the strategist, the counselor, the spiritual advisor, and the logistics manager all in one. All while telling myself: *"This is what a good leader does."*

How Burnout Shows Up in an Unfinished Leader

Burnout didn't arrive in my life with a label. It crept in as:

Constant fatigue.

Irritability.

Loss of joy in things I used to love.

Resentment toward the very people I wanted to serve.

Numbness—just going through the motions.

Sometimes I did not realize I was burning out until my body and emotions forced me to pay attention. Burnout is what happens when your will keeps saying "yes" while your soul is quietly waving a white flag.

Learning to Ask: "What Is Actually Mine to Carry?"

One of the most powerful questions I've learned to ask is: *"What is actually mine to carry here?"*

As a leader, there are things that truly are yours:

Your integrity.

Your decisions.

Your preparation.

Your attitude.

Your boundaries.

But there are things that are not yours:

Other adults' refusal to grow.

Other people's feelings about every decision you make.

Every crisis in every person's life.

The entire weight of an institution, family, or community.

An unfinished leader learns to differentiate: What is mine to carry? What is ours to carry? And What is God's (or life's) to carry?

Reflection: Where Are You Over-Responsible?

Ask yourself: *Where do I feel most tired and resentful right now?*

In that area, what am I carrying that no one asked me to—or that no human can carry alone?

What am I afraid will happen if I put some of that down?

PRACTICE: Put One Thing Down

This week, choose one small responsibility you can:

Delegate.

Delay.

Or drop.

It might be: Saying no to an extra committee, asking a family member to share a household task or letting a competent colleague fully own a project.

You are not being selfish.

You are being sustainable.

An unfinished leader plans to be here for the long journey, not just the next crisis. Burnout, overresponsibility, and the lie of "I can handle it" do not just live in your calendar. They live in your nervous system. They live in your marriage. They live in your relationship with God. They live in the way your children look at you when you come home. They live in the way you talk to yourself when the house is quiet, and the emails are finally done.

This is not theoretical. This is where unfinished leaders either learn a new way—or quietly disappear.

When "I Can Handle It" Becomes "I Don't Feel Anything"

Burnout rarely starts with a dramatic collapse. It starts with small betrayals of yourself that you call *"no big deal"*: You say yes to a late meeting even though you promised your child you'd be at their game. You take on another project because "there's no one else," even though you're already sleepdeprived. You answer emails at midnight because "this is just a season," but the season never ends. At first, you still feel it.

You feel:

The sting of missing moments.

The heaviness of another obligation.

The quiet anger that no one seems to notice how much you're carrying.

Then, slowly, the feelings dull.

The anger turns into a lowgrade irritability.

The sadness turns into numbness.

You are not fine.

You are functioning.

There is a difference.

STORY: The Morning I Realized I'd Gone Numb

One Sunday, I sat in church with my family. The worship team was singing a song that used to make me cry every time. It was about God's faithfulness, about being carried through storms. I remembered the first time I heard it— standing in my kitchen, tears streaming down my face, hands lifted over a sink full of dishes.

That morning, I felt...nothing. I sang the words. My mouth moved. My hands clapped at the right times. Inside, it was like someone had turned the volume all the way down. I wasn't angry at God. I wasn't doubting my faith. I was just...blank. After service, people hugged me. *"Dr. A, so good to see you!"* *"You're such an inspiration." "We're praying for you; we know you're carrying a lot."*

I smiled.

I nodded.

I said, "Thank you."

Driving home, I stared at the road and thought, "I have become the strong leader they see—and I've lost touch with the woman I actually am." That numbness was not random. It was the bill for years of *"I can handle it"* without rest, without help, without honest lament. My soul had gone into conservation mode. For me, unfinished leadership began when I stopped treating numbness as "just being busy." I started seeing it as a warning light:

"You are losing access to your own heart."

The Family That Paid for My "Yes"

Over-responsibility is not just a personal problem. It has a ripple effect.

Every time you say, *"I'll handle it,"* someone else doesn't get to. Every time you say yes to one thing, you are saying no to something else. Often, the *"no"* lands on the people closest to you.

STORY: The Dinner Table with an Empty Chair

There was a stretch when I was leading an institution, growing a school, teaching, and managing a full household. Evenings were a blur:

Meetings that ran late. Calls that "couldn't wait." Events I felt I "had" to attend. One night, I rushed home after a long board meeting. I walked in, still on a call, laptop bag on my shoulder. From the corner of my eye, I saw the table:

Plates.	Cups.
Food half-eaten.	My chair...empty.

I finished the call in the bedroom, closed the door, and leaned against it. I could hear my family in the other room—dishes clinking, kids laughing, the TV on. I had missed dinner. Again. My default script tried to jump in: "This is what it takes." "They'll understand." "You're doing this for them." Another voice, quieter but more honest, said:

"They are getting your income. They are not getting you."

Later that week, one of my kids drew a picture for a school project. It was our family around the table. I was drawn in—on the phone. I smiled at first. Then I looked closer. Everyone else was looking at each other. My little stick-figure self was turned away. I asked, half-joking, "Is that really how you see me?" My child shrugged. "You're always busy, Mom," they said. "You're here, but you're not...here." The words landed like a stone. I had been so busy carrying everyone that I was slowly disappearing from my own life. Unfinished leadership meant I had to tell the truth:

"I am not the only one paying for my over-responsibility. My people are paying too."

That realization hurt more than any performance review ever could. It pushed me to start asking, not just, "Can I handle it?" but: "Should I?" "At what cost?" "To whom?"

When "Helping" Becomes a Way to Avoid Yourself

Over-responsible leaders often look very selfless.

Always available.

Always serving.

Always doing.

But sometimes, the constant helping is less about love—and more about escape. If you are always tending to other people's crises, you never have to sit still long enough to face your own.

STORY: The Leader Who Didn't Know What She Liked Anymore

A woman came to me once, exhausted. She was a leader in her church, a go-to volunteer, the person everyone called when something needed to be done. "I don't understand," she said. "I'm doing so much for God, for my family, for my community, but I feel empty. Is that selfish?" We talked about her week; every hour was accounted for.

Work.

Ministry.

Kids.

Parents.

Errands.

I asked, "When was the last time you did something simply because it brought you joy?" She stared at me, confused. "What do you mean?" she asked. "Something not for productivity. Not for anyone else. Not to check a box. Just...because you like it."

She was quiet for a longtime, and then tears filled her eyes. "I don't know," she whispered. "I don't even know what I like anymore."

Her life had become a series of responses to other people's needs. She had forgotten that she was a person with a soul, not a machine with a to-do list.er over-responsibility was a shield. As long as she was busy with everyone else's problems, she never had to ask:

"What am I feeling?"

"What do I need?"

"What do I want?"

Unfinished leadership invites you to see this pattern for what it is:

Not pure sacrifice, but avoidance. Avoidance of your own grief. Your own disappointment. Your own desire. Your own questions for God. Facing those things is scary. So, you keep moving. Keep fixing. Keep handling. Until your body, your relationships, or your spirit force you to stop.

The Body Keeps the Score (Even When You're "Fine")

Burnout is not just emotional; it is physical. Your body has been carrying your "I can handle it" long before your mind admits there's a problem. You might notice:

Headaches, that have become "normal."

Back pain that never really goes away.

Stomach issues, that flare up during stressful seasons.

Insomnia—or the opposite, wanting to sleep all the time.

You tell yourself: "I just need vitamins." "I just need a weekend." "I just need a better mattress. "Maybe. Or maybe your body is telling the truth your mouth won't say.

STORY: The Day My Body Sat Me Down

There was a week when I had stacked my schedule beyond reason. Early morning prayer calls. Full workdays. Evening meetings. Weekend events. By Friday, I was moving on autopilot. That afternoon, I was walking down a hallway, thinking about the next meeting, when everything went blurry. The walls tilted, and my ears rang. I grabbed the railing and slid down to the floor, heart pounding.

People rushed over, asking, "Are you okay?"

"I'm fine," I tried to say, but my voice sounded far away.

Paramedics were called. They checked my blood pressure, which was normal, but still didn't feel good. One of them looked at me and asked, "Have you been under a lot of stress?"

I almost laughed. "Is there another kind?" I wanted to say. Later, sitting in the ER, wired to machines, I felt a strange combination of fear and shame.

Fear that my body was breaking. Shame that I had let it get this far. I heard that familiar inner lecture:

"You know better."

"You write and teach about this."

"How did you end up here again?"

Then another thought came, softer and more kind:

"Your body did what you would not. It made you stop."

From that day, I began to treat physical symptoms as data, not inconveniences. The headache when I thought about a certain meeting. The knot in my stomach before saying yes to a new commitment. The tightness in my chest when my calendar filled with no white space. Unfinished leadership is not just spiritual and emotional work. *It is bodily.* It means honoring the God-designed limits of your humanity. Not because you are weak. *Because you are finite.*

The Guilt That Shows Up When You Try to Rest

If you've lived in over-responsibility for a long time, rest will not feel natural at first. It will feel wrong. You will sit down and immediately think of ten things you "should" be doing. You will put your phone in another room and feel phantom vibrations. You will lie in bed and hear a chorus of inner accusations:

"You're being lazy."

"Other people don't have the luxury of resting."

"If you don't answer now, you'll let people down."

This is not evidence that you shouldn't rest. It is evidence that you have built your sense of worth on being needed.

STORY: The Saturday I Tried to Take Off

I decided once—after a particularly brutal season—that I would take one full Saturday off. No email. No school tasks. No church meetings.

Just rest.

I announced it to my family. I even put it on the calendar like an appointment. Saturday morning arrived. I woke up...and immediately reached for my phone. There were messages. **Needs. Questions.**

I felt that familiar tug.

"Just a few minutes," I thought. "Just to make sure nothing is on fire."

An hour later, I was deep in work. My "day off" was evaporating in a haze of urgency. My husband walked by and raised an eyebrow. "I thought you were off today," he said gently. I opened my mouth to explain.

To justify.

To defend.

Then I closed it. He was right.

I closed the laptop. Again.

Sat on the couch. Again.

This time, I put the phone in another room.

For the next two hours, I felt restless and useless.

I wandered around the house, picking things up, putting them down. My body didn't know what to do with stillness. I almost gave up. Then, slowly, something shifted. I noticed the quiet. I heard the sound of my children laughing in another room. I realized I hadn't heard that sound without multitasking in weeks.

We ended up spending the afternoon together—no agenda, no productivity, just being. That night, lying in bed, I thought: *"If this feels this foreign, how long have I been gone from my own life?"* Rest will not feel comfortable at first.

It will feel like withdrawal. Withdrawal from adrenaline. From validation. From the drug of being indispensable.

Unfinished leadership means you keep practicing anyway, until your nervous system learns that rest is not danger. *It is home.*

When Over-Responsibility is Spiritualized

In many faith spaces, especially for women and leaders of color, over-responsibility gets baptized. We use spiritual language to justify what is, in reality, self-neglect. We say:

"I'm just laying my life down."

"I'll rest in heaven."

"The harvest is plentiful."

"If I don't do it, who will?"

We quote verses about sacrifice and service.

We forget the ones about Sabbath, limits, and being a body with many members. We forget that even Jesus: Slept in a storm. Walked away from crowds. Left people unhealed to go to the next town. Took naps in boats.

STORY: The Prayer That Exposed My Motive

There was a night I was up late, working on a project for the school and responding to messages from people in crisis.

I was exhausted.

I prayed, "Lord, give me strength to keep going. I'll do whatever You need. Just use me."

It sounded holy. It sounded surrendered. Inside, something felt...off. I sensed a question whisper back:

"Do you want to serve Me—or do you want to be needed?"

I didn't like that question. I wanted to argue. Of course I wanted to serve God. Didn't my schedule prove it? But if I was honest, there was a part of me that was deeply afraid of not being essential. I had built so much of my identity on being the one who could handle it all. Who was I if I wasn't carrying everyone? Unfinished leadership meant repenting not just of obvious sins, but of hidden motives:

My addiction to being the hero.

My pride in being "stronger than most."

My subtle belief that God's work would fall apart if I ever lay down.

Slowly, my prayer began to change. From: "Use me until I'm empty." To:

"Use me within the limits You designed for me. Show me when to step in and when to step back. Teach me to trust that You are God when I am sleeping, not just when I am striving."

PRACTICE: A "What's Mine / What's Ours / What's God's" Inventory

When you feel overwhelmed by responsibility, try this simple written exercise. Pick one area that feels heavy right now:

Your job.	Your church role.
Your family.	A particular relationship.

Draw three columns: Mine to carry. Ours to carry. God's to carry. Then list items under each. For example, in a leadership role:

Mine to carry:

Preparing well for meetings.

Making decisions with integrity.

Communicating clearly.

Honoring my limits.

Ours to carry (team/board/family):

Implementing decisions together.

Sharing the emotional load.

Giving feedback.

God's to carry:

Outcomes beyond our control.

People's deepest heart changes.

The future of the institution.

You may discover you've been trying to drag items from the "God's" and "Ours" columns back into yours. Gently put them down.

Pray something like:

"God, I release to You what is Yours. I will be faithful with what is mine. And I will invite others to carry what is ours."

This is not abandoning responsibility. ***It is right-sizing it.***

The Quiet Bravery of Stepping Back

Sometimes, the most courageous thing an over-responsible leader can do is step back:

From a role.

From a committee.

From being the first one to volunteer.

From being the emotional center of every space.

This is terrifying. You will wonder: "Will everything fall apart?" "Will they be okay without me?" "Who am I if I'm not doing this?" And, perhaps the most vulnerable question:

"If I am not needed, will I still be wanted?"

STORY: The Committee I Finally Left

There was a committee I had been on for years. It started as a joy. Over time, it became a drain. The meetings were long. The work crept into evenings. I found myself dreading it. But I stayed because:

"They need my perspective."

"I don't want to let them down."

"What if they think I don't care?"

One day, sitting in yet another meeting, I watched the faces around the table.

Capable.

Wise.

Committed.

A thought dropped into my spirit:

"They will be okay without you. You are not the only adult in this room."

It was almost insulting. But also...freeing. I realized I had been holding on, in part, because it made me feel important. I drafted an email to the chair:

"After much thought and prayer, I believe it's time for me to step off this committee. I'm grateful for the work we've done together. I trust that strong leadership remains at this table."

I hit send with my heart pounding. I expected disappointment. Maybe even guilt-tripping. The response came:

"Thank you for all you've contributed. We'll miss your voice, but we bless your decision. Take care of yourself."

That was it. The earth didn't shake. The organization didn't crumble. They found someone else. Life moved on. And in the space that opened up, I found: More time with my family. More space for my own soul. More energy for the assignments that were truly mine. Stepping back did not make me less of a leader. It made me a more honest one.

You Are Allowed to Be Human and Still Be Called

Burnout and over-responsibility whisper:

"You don't get to be tired."

"You don't get to be human."

"You don't get to be unfinished."

They tell you that your calling and your humanity are in conflict. The Unfinished Leader tells a different story: *Your limits are not a flaw; they are part of your design. Your need for rest, help, and support is not a sign you're weak; it's a sign you're alive. Your value is not measured by how much you can carry without collapsing.*

You can be:

Deeply committed and still say, "I can't take that on right now."

Deeply faithful and still need a nap, a counselor, a break.

You are deeply called, and the journey of defining sustainable leadership for yourself is ongoing.

The people you lead do not need a martyr. They need a model. Someone who shows them what it looks like to love God, love people, and love themselves enough to still be standing ten years from now. Someone who can say:

"I used to believe that being a good leader meant handling everything. Now I know it means discerning what is mine, what is ours, and what is God's—and having the courage to put the rest down."

You do not have to earn your right to rest.

You do not have to prove your worth by how much you suffer.

You are allowed to be here for the long journey, not just the next crisis.

You are allowed to be unfinished and still lead.

CHAPTER 8

Conflict, Criticism, and the Fear of Disappointing People

If you love conflict, this chapter may not be for you. If you secretly want everyone to be happy with you at all times, pull up a chair. I used to think being a "good" leader meant:

Avoiding conflict.

Softening hard truths.

Keeping the peace at all costs.

The problem is peace without truth is not actually peace. It's just quiet tension.

My Relationship with Conflict

In different seasons of my life, conflict has felt dangerous. As a firstborn, I didn't want to rock the boat. As a divorced woman, I had already lived through relational pain. As a leader in organizations, I knew conflict could cost jobs, relationships, or reputation. So sometimes I:

Delayed hard conversations.

Hinted instead of being clear.

Took the blame to keep the peace.

Over-explained my decisions, hoping no one would be upset.

This looked loving. It felt spiritual. It was, often, fear.

Criticism: When Feedback Feels Like a Personal Attack

Let's be honest: criticism can hurt. A student evaluation that stings. A staff member who questions your leadership. A family member who doesn't agree with your choices. A social media comment that misjudges your motives. When you are an unfinished leader, criticism can confirm your worst inner story: *"See? You really are not enough."*

So you either:

Defend yourself fiercely.

Retreat and shrink.

I have done both. Learning to Stand in the Middle An unfinished leader learns to stand in the uncomfortable middle:

Not attacking back.

Not disappearing.

Listening for what is true.

Releasing what is not.

I've had to learn to say things like:

"Thank you for sharing that. Let me think about it."

"I see your perspective, even if I don't agree."

"I made a mistake there, and I'm sorry."

"I hear your feelings, but I still believe this decision is right."

This is not easy.

It *is* necessary.

Reflection: Your Conflict Style

Ask yourself:

When conflict arises, do I tend to: fight, flee, freeze, or fawn (people-please)?

How did my family of origin handle conflict? (Yelling, silence, avoidance, open discussion?)

How is that pattern showing up in my leadership today?

PRACTICE: One Clear, Kind Conversation

This week, identify one conversation you have been avoiding. Prepare:

What is the truth you need to share?

What is the outcome you hope for?

How can you speak clearly and kindly?

Then, have the conversation. You are not responsible for the other person's entire reaction. You are responsible for your clarity and your kindness. That is unfinished leadership, growing up. Conflict, criticism, and the fear of disappointing people don't just live in our homes and churches. They live in staff meetings, performance reviews, Slack channels, Zoom calls, boardrooms, break rooms, and group texts.

They sound different depending on where you sit in the organization: Conflict, criticism, and the fear of disappointing people are not side issues in leadership. They are daily, lived realities. If you have ever lost sleep replaying a hard conversation, delayed sending an email because you didn't want to "cause trouble," or over-explained a decision hoping to soften the blow—you are in the right chapter. This is where a lot of unfinished leaders either grow or get stuck.

The Quiet Ways We Trade Truth for Approval

Most of us don't wake up and say, "Today I will betray myself to keep people happy." The trade is subtler. We say:

"It's not worth the drama."

"I don't want to hurt their feelings."

"Maybe I'm overreacting."

"I'll bring it up next time."

So we:

Let a disrespectful comment pass, again.

Say yes to a request we know we should decline.

Avoid naming a pattern that is harming the team.

Pretend we're not bothered, when we are.

On the surface, everything is calm. Underneath, resentment grows. You smile in the meeting. You vent in the car. You "keep the peace" publicly. You rage in private.

Unfinished leaders eventually have to face a hard truth:

Every time I choose artificial peace over honest clarity, I plant a seed of future conflict.

The bill always comes due. Sometimes in your health. Sometimes in your relationships. Sometimes in your leadership credibility.

STORY: The Conflict I Ignored Until It Exploded

There was a staff member I'll call "Maria." Smart. Gifted. Passionate. She also had a habit of: Coming late to meetings. Dominating discussions. Making side comments when she disagreed. The first few times, I told myself: "She's just enthusiastic." "She's under a lot of stress." "I don't want to crush her spirit."

So, I said nothing. Other staff began to notice. People rolled their eyes when she spoke. They started checking out in meetings. The culture was shifting, and not in a healthy direction. I felt it. I didn't want to deal with it. The unfinished part of me thought:

"If I bring this up, she'll be hurt. She might quit. People might see me as harsh. Better to just 'manage around' her."

So I tried to:

Redirect conversations.

Do more one-on-one with others to balance her influence.

Avoid topics that might trigger her reactions.

It worked—until it didn't.

One day, in a meeting, she interrupted another staff member midsentence and said, "We've tried that before. It never works." Her tone was dismissive, her body language loud. I saw the hurt on the other staff member's face. Something in me snapped. I heard myself say, sharper than I meant:

"Maria, that's enough. You've been undermining ideas all morning. If you can't be constructive, you can be quiet."

The room went silent. She flushed. Tears sprang to her eyes. The meeting limped to a close. Afterward, I felt sick. I had finally addressed the issue—but in the worst possible way. Not thoughtfully, privately, and early. Reactively, publicly, and late.

When we met later in my office, she was hurt and defensive. *"Why didn't you say something sooner if this was a problem?"* she asked.

I didn't have a good answer. I had been so afraid of disappointing her that I had delayed the very conversation that could have helped her grow. My silence had set us both up for a harder fall. Unfinished leadership meant I had to own it.

"I should have talked with you about this weeks ago," I said. "That's on me. I let it build up instead of addressing it early. I'm sorry for how I spoke in the meeting. And we still need to talk about the pattern."

We did. It wasn't easy. Some behaviors changed. Some didn't. Eventually, she moved on to another role. The team culture healed. I carried the lesson: Avoiding conflict doesn't prevent pain. It usually multiplies it.

When Criticism Hits an Old Wound

Not all criticism is created equal. Some of it is:

Fair.　　　　Needed.　　　　A gift.

Some of it is:

Unfair.　　　　Projection.　　　　About someone else's unhealed story.

But even accurate criticism can feel devastating if it lands on an old wound.

STORY: The Email That Kept Me Up All Night

One semester, I received an email from a parent about my role at the school. It said, in part:

"I expected more from someone in your position. Your decision shows poor judgment, and I'm concerned about your leadership."

Objectively, it was one email. One person. It was firm, not abusive. But it found the twelveyearold in me who had been told:

"You should have known better."

"You're the oldest, you're responsible."

It found the divorced woman in me who had heard:

"If you had done things differently, maybe this wouldn't have happened."

It found the Black woman in me who had been scrutinized more harshly in leadership spaces. My body reacted before my brain could explain:

Tight chest. Racing thoughts. Replay, replay, replay.

I drafted three different responses:

Overexplaining every detail of my decision (to prove I wasn't incompetent). Apologizing profusely for things that weren't actually wrong (to soothe their disappointment). A sharp, defensive reply (to push back against the tone). None of them felt right. So I did something that unfinished leaders learn to do: ***I paused.***

I let myself feel what I felt. I named it:

"I feel attacked."

"I feel misunderstood."

"I feel like a child being scolded."

Then I asked:

"What part of this email is actually about my leadership today?"

"What part is waking up old shame?"

When I separated them, I could see:

There was a legitimate concern I needed to address.

There was also a layer of anxiety and tone that was not mine to fix.

My reply ended up being simple:

"Thank you for taking the time to share your concerns. I can see why this decision felt troubling from your perspective. Here is what I was weighing when I made it... Looking back, I can see some things I would do differently, and I'm sorry for the impact this had on your family. I'm committed to learning from this."

I did not beg for their approval, attack their character, or dismiss their feelings.

They wrote back later:

"Thank you for your thoughtful response. I may not agree with every choice, but I respect your willingness to listen."

The more unfinished work you do on your own story, the less power other people's criticism has to define you. It can still sting. It doesn't have to sink you.

The Fear of Disappointing People You Love

It's one thing to disappoint a stranger on the internet. It's another to disappoint:

A mentor who opened doors for you.

A pastor who prayed you into your role.

A spouse or parent who sacrificed for your dream.

A community that sees you as their "success story."

Sometimes, growth will take you in directions that don't match other people's expectations. You will have to choose: The path God and your integrity are pointing you toward, or the version of you that keeps everyone else comfortable.

STORY: The Ministry Role I Had to Say No To

There was a ministry opportunity that, on paper, looked perfect. A platform to speak. Influence in a space I cared about. The affirmation of people I respected. My mentors were excited. "This is God," they said. "You can't say no to this." Inside, I felt a knot. I was already stretched thin. My family needed more of me. My body was sending signals. In prayer, I sensed a clear but uncomfortable directive:

"Not this. Not now."

I wrestled.

Saying "no" felt like: Wasting an opportunity. Letting people down. Being ungrateful. When I finally declined, the leader who had invited me was gracious but surprised. "Are you sure?" he asked. "This doesn't come around often." I wasn't "sure" in the way I hoped to be.

I was shaky. I was secondguessing. I was grieving the image of myself on that stage. But I was convinced enough. "Yes," I said. "I need to prioritize my current assignments and my health." Some people understood. Some did not. A few implied, gently or not so gently, that I was missing God. For a while, their voices were louder than my own. Then, months later, a series of intense crises hit in the places I was already leading. If I had added that ministry role, something would have broken:

My health.

My marriage.

My integrity.

Saying no had created margin I didn't know I would need. Disappointing those leaders was painful. But it was holy. Unfinished leadership sometimes looks like:

"I will grieve your disappointment, but I will not betray myself or my family to avoid it."

When You Are the One Who Hurt Someone

It's easier to talk about conflict when we are the misunderstood, overcriticized leader. Harder when we are the one who caused harm. Even with good intentions. Even without malice.

Unfinished leaders must learn how to handle those moments without:

Collapsing into shame.   Deflecting responsibility.   Minimizing impact.

STORY: The Comment That Cut Deeper Than I Knew

In a staff gathering, I made an offhand comment trying to lighten the mood. I said something like, "Well, you know how those departments are—always last-minute."

People laughed.

We moved on.

Later that day, one of the staff from that department asked if we could talk.

She sat in my office, eyes wet. "When you said 'those departments,'" she said, "it felt like all the work we've been doing to build trust just...disappeared. We've been trying so hard to change the perception that we're disorganized. Hearing my president joke about us like that hurt."

My first instinct was to explain:

"I didn't mean it that way."

"Everyone knew I was joking."

"You're being too sensitive."

That instinct was about my comfort, not her pain.

I took a breath.

I remembered:

My words carry weight beyond my intention.

My position amplifies my off-hand remarks. I said, *"You're right to bring this up. I was trying to be funny, and I wasn't thinking about how it would land. I'm sorry. That wasn't fair to you or your team."*

Then I asked, "Would it be helpful if I addressed that publicly with the group?" She nodded.

At our next gathering, I said to the whole staff: *"Last time we were together, I made a comment about certain departments always being lastminute. That was wrong. It reinforced a stereotype that doesn't reflect the effort and progress many of you have made. I'm sorry. I'm committed to speaking more carefully about our teams."*

It was uncomfortable. It was also necessary. Owning your impact does not make you weak. It makes you trustworthy. Unfinished leaders do not cling to the image of "always right." They are willing to say: "I was wrong. I'm learning. I will do better."

Conflict as a Teacher, Not Just a Threat

If you grew up in a home where conflict meant:

Yelling.	Stonewalling.
Silent treatment.	Violence.

Your body may interpret any disagreement as danger. Your nervous system goes into:

Fight (attack).	Flight (run).
Freeze (shut down).	Fawn (peopleplease).

Unfinished leadership doesn't shame these reactions.

It gets curious about them. "What am I afraid will happen if we really talk about this?" "Whose voice does this conflict remind me of?" "What story am I telling myself about what disagreement means?" Conflict can be a brutal teacher. It can also be a powerful one. It can reveal:

Hidden expectations.	Unspoken needs.
Misalignments in values.	Places where growth is overdue.

The goal is not to love conflict. The goal is to no longer be ruled by the fear of it.

PRACTICE: A "Hard Conversation" Map

Think of one conversation you've been avoiding. Maybe it's with:

A staff member.

A supervisor.

A spouse.

A friend.

A church member.

Take a sheet of paper and draw three columns: *What is true that I need to say?* (Facts, patterns, observations. No exaggerations.). What am I afraid will happen if I say it? (Rejection, anger, tears, loss of relationship, loss of role.). What might also be possible if I say it? (Clarity, healing, boundary, mutual understanding, a better path.). Then, below the columns, write a simple script that starts like this:

"I care about you and about this relationship/this team. There's something I've been holding back because I didn't want to upset you. But I realize staying silent isn't fair to either of us. Can we talk about it?" You may never say it exactly that way. But mapping it out lowers the emotional temperature. You move from vague dread to a specific, intentional step. That is unfinished leadership in motion.

You Will Disappoint People. The Question Is: Who?

If you try to avoid disappointing anyone, you will end up disappointing: Yourself. Your Calling.. Often, the people who actually needed your honesty. You are going to disappoint someone. The question is not if. The question is who and for what.

Will you disappoint a colleague by telling them "no," or disappoint your children by constantly telling them "maybe next time"?

Will you disappoint a supervisor by holding a boundary, or disappoint your own body by pushing past its limits?

Will you disappoint a congregation by not being available 24/7, or disappoint your marriage by never really being home?

Unfinished leadership requires brutal clarity:

"I am willing to disappoint people in service of what is right, true, and sustainable. I am not willing to betray my deepest values to avoid short-term discomfort."

This doesn't make you harsh. It makes you clear. And clarity, even when it disappoints, is kinder than false promises.

STORY: The Congregant I Couldn't Be Everything For

A woman in our faith community once called me late at night, again and again. She was in genuine distress.

Lonely.   Anxious.   Afraid.

I took the calls—for a while. Listened. Prayed. Encouraged. But the calls increased. Midnight. Early mornings. She would text, "I need you. You're the only one who understands." Something in me felt important. *Needed.* Something in me also felt trapped. My family was losing me to someone else's endless midnight.

One day, after a string of sleepless nights, my husband gently said, *"I love your heart. I also miss my wife."* I knew something had to change. I met with her during the day.

"I care about you," I said. *"I also have limits. I can't be your only support. I'm not available for latenight calls anymore, but I want to help you build a wider circle. Can we talk about other resources—counseling, small group, trusted friends?"*

She was hurt. "I thought you were different," she said. "I thought you were my pastor."

The old me would have doubled down, overexplained, tried to prove I still cared enough. The unfinished me felt the sting and held the boundary. "I am your pastor," I said. "And because I am, I need to lead you toward healthy community, not just toward me. I'm not abandoning you. I'm changing how I show up so that I can still be here longterm."

She pulled back for a while. Eventually, she did connect with others. Our relationship changed, becoming healthier. She no longer saw me as her personal 24/7 rescue line. I no longer saw myself as her savior. I disappointed her shortterm. I honored us both longterm.

You Can Be Gentle and Unshakeable

If you're reading this chapter, you probably value kindness. You don't want to be the kind of leader who: Steamrolls people. Dismisses feelings. Uses authority as a weapon. *Good.* We have enough of those. But gentleness does not mean:

Never saying "no."

Never making firm decisions.

Never causing discomfort.

Jesus was gentle. He also turned over tables. Paul wrote about love. He also confronted Peter publicly when his behavior harmed the community. Gentleness and strength are not opposites. They are siblings. Unfinished leadership is learning to hold both:

A soft heart.

A strong spine.

You can say: "I love you. And the answer is no." "I understand you're upset. And I'm still making this decision." "I value your feedback. And I see it differently." Without: **Attacking. Collapsing. Apologizing for existing.**

You Are Not the Villain for Having a Voice

If you grew up in environments where:

Speaking up was labeled "rebellion."

Asking questions was seen as disrespect.

Saying no was called selfish. Then stepping into honest conflict will feel, at first, like you're doing something wrong. You're not. You are learning to be a whole person. You will make mistakes. You will say too much one day, not enough the next. You will misread someone's readiness. You will sometimes wish you could take your words back. That does not mean you should go back to silence. It means you are practicing. It means you are unfinished. Over time, with God's help and wise support, you will grow in:

Timing.   Tone.   Discernment.   Courage.

And you will discover something surprising: Some of your most meaningful relationships and most impactful leadership moments will come through conflict you were once terrified to face. People will say things like:

"That conversation was hard, but I respect you more because you had it."

Thank you for telling me the truth when it would have been easier to stay quiet. I didn't like what you said at first. Now I see it helped me grow.

You are not the villain for having a voice.

You are not the villain for having boundaries.

You are not the villain for making decisions that some people dislike.

You are an unfinished leader, learning to love people enough to tell them the truth—and to let them have their own feelings about it.

That is not the end of your leadership. That is the beginning of its growth. Whether at the top (as a CEO or senior leader), in the middle (as a manager or director), or on the front line (dealing with customers, students, patients, or congregants every day), the unfinished leader has to learn how to face conflict and criticism from each of these vantage points—without becoming hard, fake, or invisible. Below are three angles on the same struggle.

1. From the Top: The CEO Who Wants Everyone to Like Her

When you are the CEO, president, senior pastor, or founder, conflict changes shape. You are no longer just managing your own preferences. You are stewarding Budgets. Jobs. Families. Reputations. Futures. Your decisions land on real people. Some of them will not be happy. Even when you do what is right. Especially when you do what is right.

The Temptation to Lead by Consensus (Even When You Shouldn't)

A CEO I'll call Angela led a mid-sized nonprofit. She loved her team. She cared deeply about being a "relational" leader. When major decisions came up, she did what many of us would do: She asked for input, She listened to concerns, She tried to find the option everyone could live with. On the surface, this looked healthy. Underneath, something else was happening. Her fear of disappointing people made her:

Delay hard decisions about underperforming staff.

Avoid restructuring that everyone knew was needed.

Soften feedback until it lost its meaning.

Add more and more "exceptions" to policies to keep individuals happy. Her leadership team started to feel it. One of them finally said in a private meeting:

"We love that you care about people. But we're starting to feel like the mission is being held hostage by everyone's feelings—including ours."

That sentence pierced her. She realized she had been treating disappointment as failure—hers and theirs. So she overcorrected by trying to make everyone "okay" all the time. The cost? Confusion.

Resentment from high performers. Burnout for herself.

STORY: The Layoff Conversation That Broke My Heart

I remember a season, as a president, when we had to make painful budget cuts. Numbers did not care how kind I was. We had exhausted every soft option. We had trimmed where we could. The math still told the truth:

We could not keep every role. We could not keep every program.

The unfinished part of me wanted to "figure out a way" that simply didn't exist. Avoid being the face of people's pain. Hide behind vague emails and passive language. I had to decide:

"Will I be honest and present in this conflict, or will I disappear to protect myself?"

We set up one-on-one meetings with those affected. I sat across from people I respected and said words no leader wants to say:

"This is not about your worth or your work ethic. This is about numbers and sustainability. I am so sorry."

Some cried. Some were angry. Some were quiet. I felt every reaction in my body. I drove home after one of those days, pulled into a parking lot, and sobbed. It would have been easier to let someone else deliver the news. But true leadership meant:

I did not pretend this wasn't happening.

I did not spin it as "an exciting opportunity."

I held my own grief and theirs at the same time.

Not everyone understood. Some will always connect my name to that hard season. I had to make peace with that. Because my job was not to avoid all disappointment. It was to tell the truth, as gently and clearly as I could, and carry my part of the cost.

The CEO's Inner Work in Conflict

If you are at the top, ask yourself: Where am I over-identifying with being "the nice boss" instead of being a truthful one? Where am I delaying necessary change because I don't want to be the reason someone is upset? Where am I confusing "everyone agrees" with "this is the right decision"? Practice one CEO-level sentence this week that is both clear and kind:

"I know this isn't the outcome you were hoping for. I care about you and your contribution. And after weighing everything, this is the decision I believe is best for the organization."

You will feel the pull to apologize for disappointing people. You do not need to apologize for doing your job with integrity. You can apologize for how you deliver truth if you fail there—not for having to deliver it.

2. From the Middle: The Manager Caught Between "Them" and "Us"

Middle managers live in a unique kind of conflict. They are:

Accountable up to senior leadership. Responsible down to their direct reports. Stuck in the middle when decisions are unpopular.

They hear:

From above: "Make it happen.", "We need buy-in.", "Why is your team resisting?"

From below: "They don't understand what it's like down here.". "Why are you doing this to us?", "We thought you were on our side."

The Temptation to Over-Identify with One Side

A manager I'll call Jamal oversaw a team in a company that was going through a major restructure. Senior leadership rolled out new metrics and systems. His team was overwhelmed. They vented to him:

"This is unrealistic."

"They don't care about our workload."

"We're just numbers to them."

Jamal agreed with many of their concerns. He also knew some of the bigger picture that they didn't see: Financial pressures. Industry shifts. Legal constraints.

He felt torn. To his team, he wanted to say, "You're right, this is awful." To his bosses, he wanted to say, "You're pushing too hard."

Instead, he did what many middle managers do: He tried to be "neutral" in front of everyone. He said to the team:

"Well, this is the direction, so let's do our best."

He said to leadership:

"They're on board. Just some minor concerns."

He thought he was keeping the peace. In reality, he was eroding trust on both sides. His team felt: *Unseen. Unheard. Slightly betrayed.*

His leaders felt: *Misled.*

Surprised when resistance showed up later.

STORY: The Performance Review I Dreaded Giving

I remember sitting in my office as a dean with a performance review in my hand. My supervisor had been clear:

"This person is not meeting expectations. We need to see improvement, or we have to consider other options."

The staff member was kind. Faithful. Loved by students. However, they also: Missed deadlines. Struggled with follow-through. Avoided difficult tasks.

I liked them. I knew they were trying. I also knew the impact on the team. The unfinished part of me wanted to soften everything:

"You're doing great, just a few tiny tweaks."

The honest part knew that would be a disservice. I sat across from them, my heart racing, and chose a third way:

"There are things you're doing very well. Students feel safe with you. Your presence matters here. And there are also specific areas where your performance is not meeting expectations. If these don't change, it will affect your role." They looked stunned. "No one ever told me it was that serious," they said. My stomach turned. I realized: in previous check-ins, I had been too vague. Trying not to hurt them, I had failed to help them. We spent the rest of the meeting mapping out:

Clear expectations. Concrete steps.

Support they would need. A timeline. They didn't love the conversation. They also later said, *"Thank you for finally being straight with me. It was scary, but it gave me a chance to actually change."*

The Manager's Inner Work in Conflict

If you are in the middle, ask yourself: Where am I trying so hard to be liked by my team that I'm not delivering the clarity they need? Where am I trying so hard to be liked by senior leaders that I'm not telling them the truth from the frontlines? Where do I need to stop being "neutral" and start being honest about what I see? Practice one "bridge" sentence this week that honors both directions:

To your team:

"I hear your frustration, and it makes sense. I also see some of the pressures leadership is facing. Let's talk together about what we can control, what we need to push back on, and how we can make this as humane as possible."

To your leaders:

"My team is committed to the mission, but they are at or near capacity. If we move forward with this timeline, here's the likely cost; if we adjust it, here's what could help."

You will feel afraid of disappointing both sides. You might. That doesn't make you a bad manager. It makes you an honest one.

3. From the Front Line: The Everyday Conflicts No One Sees

Frontline workers—teachers, nurses, receptionists, customer service reps, youth leaders, assistants, coordinators—live in constant, lowgrade conflict. They hold: The complaints. The confusion. The misdirected anger at policies they didn't make. They are often: *Underpaid. Overworked. Overlooked.* And yet they are the "face" of the organization to the people it serves.

STORY: The Front Desk and the Furious Parent

A frontdesk coordinator, I'll call Leah worked at a school. One afternoon, a parent stormed into the office. They were angry about a decision the administration had made. *"You people don't care about our kids!"* they shouted.

Leah had not made the decision. She had learned about it in the same email as everyone else. But she was the one standing behind the counter. She had a choice: Absorb the attack in silence, go home, and sob. Fight back and say, *"I'm not the one who did this, calm down."*

Practice unfinished leadership from the front line.

She took a breath and said: *"I can see you're really upset. I would be, too, if I felt my child wasn't being heard. I don't have the authority to change this decision, but I do want to make sure your concerns are heard by the right people. Can we sit down for a moment so I can understand what's happening from your side?"* The parent's volume lowered a notch. They sat. They vented. She listened. She didn't promise what she couldn't deliver.

She said:

"Here's what I can do: I can document this, share it directly with the principal, and ask for a followup. Here's what I can't do: override this decision on my own today." The parent left calmer. Leah went to her car later and cried. Holding other people's emotions all day is heavy.

When I talked with her, she said:

"Sometimes I feel like a punching bag for decisions I never made. I want to represent the school well, but I also feel alone."

Frontline unfinished leadership looks like: Holding space for people's feelings. Being clear about your limits. Advocating up the chain when patterns emerge. Taking your own heart seriously instead of just "toughing it out."

When Your Supervisor Avoids Conflict—and Leaves You Exposed

Another frontliner, Chris, worked in customer service. He had a manager who hated conflict. When customers were upset, the manager often disappeared into their office, leaving Chris to absorb the heat.

If Chris asked for support, the manager would say:

"Just try to keep them happy. You're good with people."

Translation: "Handle it so I don't have to." Chris started to: Dread coming to work. Take everything personally. Fantasize about quitting.

He eventually realized:

"I can't control my manager's conflict avoidance. I can control how I advocate for myself."

He scheduled a meeting and said:

"When customers are upset and I'm the only one dealing with them, it puts me in a difficult position. I need clearer guidelines on what I can and cannot offer, and I need to know you're willing to step in when a situation escalates beyond my role."

His manager was uncomfortable.

They had to face their own avoidance. They made some changes: Clear escalation protocols. Training for the team. A commitment to be physically present when things escalated. Chris still faced conflict daily. But he no longer felt abandoned in it.

The Frontliner's Inner Work in Conflict

If you are on the front line, ask yourself: Where am I carrying conflict that belongs to someone higher up? Where do I need to ask for clearer authority and support? Where am I taking criticism personally when it's really about a broken system?

Practice saying one sentence this week that honors your humanity and your role:

"I want to help you as much as I can. Here's what I'm able to do from my position, and here's what I need to refer to my supervisor."

You are not weak for needing backup. You are not "overly sensitive" for feeling the weight of daily conflict. You are an unfinished leader in one of the hardest places to be one.

4. When Levels Collide: A Conflict Seen from Three Angles

Let's take one scenario and look at it from all three levels.

Scenario: A new policy reduces flexible work hours.

CEO: feels pressure from the board to standardize hours and improve productivity data.

Manager: knows the policy will hit parents and caregivers hardest.

Frontliner: is a parent who will now struggle with school pickup.

CEO Lens: The CEO reads the data:

Missed deadlines.

Customer complaints about availability.

Budget constraints.

She decides the organization needs more structure. She approves a stricter schedule.

Her fear: "If I don't do this, the board will think I'm not serious about performance." "If I do this, my people will feel betrayed."

Her unfinished work is to: Communicate the why clearly, acknowledge the human cost, and invite feedback on how to implement with compassion.

Manager Lens: The manager hears the policy and immediately thinks of her team:

Single parents.

Caregivers.

People with long commutes.

Her fear: "They're going to blame me.", and "I'm going to lose my best people."

Her unfinished work is to: Tell the truth about the impact to senior leadership, not throw leadership under the bus, and help her team problem-solve within the new constraints.

She might say to leadership:

"I understand the need for clearer hours. Here's how this will affect retention in my team. Are there any exceptions or supports we can build in for caregivers?"

She might say to her team:

"I know this change is hard. I didn't make the policy, but I am here to help us navigate it. Let's talk through what you're facing and what options we can explore together."

Frontliner Lens: The frontliner reads the memo and panic:

"How will I pick up my kids?", "Will I have to choose between my job and my family?"

Her fear: "If I speak up, they'll think I'm not committed.", "If I stay quiet, I'll drown."

Her unfinished work is to: Name her needs without apologizing for them. Ask about options instead of assuming there are none. Make a decision about whether this job still fits her life.

She might say to her manager:

"This new schedule is going to be really hard for me as a single parent. Are there any creative options—like shift swaps, compressed hours, or partial remote days—that we could consider? I want to stay and keep contributing, and I also need to be realistic about my family responsibilities."

Not every organization will respond well.

Not every CEO will listen.

Not every manager will advocate.

Not every frontliner will be heard.

But unfinished leadership at each level means:

You don't just stew in resentment.

You speak.

You listen.

You stay human.

5. What Grows When You Stop Running from Workplace Conflict

When CEOs, managers, and frontliners all start practicing unfinished leadership in conflict, several things change.

    A. Trust Increases, not because everyone agrees or no one gets hurt. But because: People know where they stand. Hard things are said with respect. Decisions are explained, not just announced.

B. **Burnout Decreases** when CEOs stop trying to please everyone, Managers stop carrying everyone's emotional load alone, and Frontliners stop pretending they are robots with no limits. ...people can breathe.

They can: Say "no" sometimes. Ask for help. Set boundaries without being labeled disloyal.

C. **Real Growth Becomes Possible.** You cannot grow what you cannot name. When conflict is always avoided, nothing changes. When criticism is always taken as attack or always dismissed, no one matures. When the fear of disappointing people runs the whole show, the organization stays stuck.

Unfinished leaders at every level practice:

Naming problems early.

Owning their part.

Letting others own theirs.

Staying in relationship, when possible, through the discomfort.

6. One Shared Practice for Every Level

Whether you are a CEO, a middle manager, or a frontliner, try this before your next hard conversation:

Regulate Your Body: Three slow, deep breaths. Feel your feet on the floor. Relax your shoulders.

Name Your Fear (silently or on paper): "I'm afraid they'll think I'm heartless.", "I'm afraid I'll lose my job.", "I'm afraid I'll cry."

Name Your Value: I value honesty.", "I value dignity.", "I value justice.", "I value sustainability."

Then you need to choose which one will lead: *fear or value.* Then go into the conversation with one simple internal commitment:

"I may not say everything perfectly, but I will not let fear—not of conflict, not of criticism, not of disappointing people—be the loudest voice in the room."

That is not about being finished. It is about being faithful.

In the C-suite.

In the middle.

On the floor.

In the classroom.

At the front desk.

You are allowed to be unfinished and still step into conflict with courage. You are allowed to disappoint people and still be a good leader. You are allowed to grow in this.

One hard, honest, imperfect conversation at a time.

CHAPTER 9

Soul Care:
Rest, Reflection, and Staying Human

I have led on empty. I have preached tired. I have parented exhausted. I have sat on panels depleted. It never ended well. You cannot do deep work in the world while treating your own soul like a side project.

What Happens When I Ignore My Soul

When I ignore my inner life long enough, it shows up as:

Snapping at people I love.

Numbing out with screens or busyness.

Feeling disconnected from my own joy.

Going through spiritual motions while feeling spiritually dry.

Losing creativity and compassion.

On the outside, I might still look "productive." On the inside, I am withering.

Rest Is Not a Reward

For years, I treated rest as something I would earn after I finished everything. ***Newsflash: I never finished everything.*** There was always: one more email, one more person in crisis, one more project and one more event.

I had to:

Unlearn "I rest when the work is done.", and **Relearn** "I rest so that I can keep doing the work well."

Rest is not a luxury. It is part of responsible leadership.

Simple Practices That Keep Me Human

I don't have a perfect routine, but here are some practices that help me:

Daily check-ins: 5 minutes to ask, "What am I feeling? What do I need?"

Sabbath rhythms: a regular time (even a few hours) when I do not produce, fix, or perform.

Movement: walking, stretching—anything that reminds me I have a body, not just a brain.

Honest prayer: not just "spiritual" words, but real ones: "I'm tired. I'm angry. I'm grateful. Help me."

Play and laughter: with my kids, my spouse, my friends.

These are not extra credit. They are survival.

Reflection: How Is Your Soul?

Right now, if you had to answer honestly:

How tired are you—physically, emotionally, spiritually?

What gives you life that you haven't done in a long time?

Where have you been ignoring your own needs in the name of "being a good leader"?

PRACTICE: Schedule One Act of Soul Care

This week, pick one simple act of soul care:

- Go to bed 30–60 minutes earlier one night.

- Take a 15-minute walk without your phone.

- Sit in silence for 5 minutes and breathe.

- Read something that nourishes you, not just informs you.

Put it on your calendar. Treat it like an appointment with someone important—because it is. ***You.***

Reflection and Practice Notes

PART IV

Leading Others While Still Becoming

CHAPTER 10

Leading Others from an Unfinished Place

By now, you've noticed a theme: I am not offering you a picture of a leader on a pedestal. I am inviting you to walk with a leader in process. So what does it look like to lead others from this unfinished place?

Modeling, Not Performing

People are not transformed by your perfection. They are transformed by your authentic process. As a professor, president, founder, mother, and mentor, I've seen that:

When I pretend to be perfect, people either idolize or resent me.

When I am appropriately honest, people feel safe to grow.

Leading from an unfinished place means saying, *"Here's what I'm learning,"* not just, *"Here's what you should do."*

Admitting, *"I was wrong there,"* without crumbling.

Letting your team see you change your mind when you get new information.

Creating Cultures of Grace and Growth

In my school, in my teams, and in my home, I try (imperfectly) to create cultures where:

Mistakes are for learning, not for lifelong labeling.

Feedback goes both ways.

People are allowed to grow and change.

Boundaries are respected.

Rest is honored, not shamed.

This is not soft leadership.

It is strong, humane leadership. It produces: *More creativity. More honesty. More resilience. More ownership.*

Developing Other Unfinished Leaders

One of my greatest joys now is developing other leaders through:

Teaching. Coaching. My "Why Move My Cheese" conference. Everyday mentoring in my community and family. I don't try to clone myself. I try to help people:

Understand their own story.

Notice their own masks.

Face their own fears.

Step into their own calling—unfinished.

I tell them what I'm telling you:

"You don't have to wait until you feel finished to lead. You start now, and you grow as you go."

Reflection: How Do You Show Up for Others? Ask yourself:

Do people around me feel safe to be unfinished, or do they feel pressured to perform?

How do I respond when someone on my team (or in my family) makes a mistake?

What is one way I can model growth, not perfection, this week?

PRACTICE: Share a Lesson, Not Just a Standard

This week, with someone you lead (a child, a student, a staff member), share:

A standard you uphold ("We do our work with excellence").

A story of how you learned that standard the hard way.

Show them: *"I wasn't born with this. I learned it. And you can, too."*

That's unfinished leadership in action. Leading others while you are still becoming is both the most humbling and the most sacred work you will ever do. You will stand in front of people who: Call you "Dr.," "Boss," "Pastor," "Director," "Mom," "Mentor"...

Expect you to know what you're doing. Assume you've worked it all out. And there you'll be—heart still healing, questions still swirling, triggers still firing, story still unfolding. The finished leader pretends that is not true.

The unfinished leader tells the truth—and leads anyway.

When People Want a Hero and Get a Human

Most groups, whether they say it out loud or not, are looking for a hero. "Fix our problems.", "Carry our hopes.", "Be better than the leaders who hurt us before.", They project onto you: *Their unmet needs. Their old disappointments. Their fantasies of "the one" who will finally get it right.* You feel it when you walk into a room:

The quiet expectation.

The eager eyes.

The weight of being "the one in charge."

If you are not careful, you will start trying to be the thing they imagine: Stronger than you feel. Wiser than you are. Less human than you'll ever be.

STORY: The Night I Realized They Were Watching My Life, Not Just My Work

Years ago, after a long day on campus, I was leaving late. Lights were low. Hallways mostly empty. As I walked out, I saw a small knot of students by the door, talking quietly. They saw me and straightened. "Good night, Dr. A!" they called. I smiled, waved, and kept going. As I passed, I heard one of them whisper, *"She's always so put together."* I almost laughed out loud. Ten minutes earlier, I had been in my office:

Shoes off.

Head in my hands.

Fighting tears over a difficult email.

I thought, "If only you knew."

Driving home, it hit me: "They're not just watching what I do. They're watching how I am."

How I respond when things go wrong.

How I treat people who can't give me anything.

How I talk about those who criticize me.

How I show up when I'm tired.

They were building a picture of "leadership" from my life, not just my résumé. That realization did not make me want to perform more. It made me want to be more honest. Because if they only ever saw the polished version, they would grow up believing:

"Real leaders don't struggle."

"Real leaders don't cry."

"Real leaders never doubt."

I did not want to pass that lie on.

The Myth of "Once I'm Over This, Then I'll Lead"

A common fantasy sounds like this: "Once I'm healed...Once the kids are older...Once I'm not afraid anymore...Then I'll really step into leadership. "You imagine a future version of yourself:

Unbothered by criticism.

Fully confident in every room.

Completely free from insecurity or old wounds.

You tell yourself you owe it to others to wait until you are that person. But life does not pause for your perfection. Assignments arrive while:

You are still going to therapy.

You are still learning boundaries.

You are still figuring out how to rest.

God, life, and community keep asking:

"Will you teach this class?"

"Will you lead this team?"

"Will you plant this ministry?"

"Will you mentor this young person?"

Not because you are finished, but because you are faithful.

STORY: The Leadership Role I Took in the Middle of My Own Mess

There was a season when my personal life was in upheaval. **Grief. Transition.** Old trauma finally coming to the surface. It was not a "sparkling" time. In the middle of that, I was asked to step into a new leadership role. My first instinct was to say no. I thought:

"I'm too broken right now."

"They need someone more stable."

"I can't pour out when I'm this empty."

I prayed, expecting a clear release. Instead, I sensed a different invitation:

"Can you lead from your need instead of from your image? Can you bring all of who you are—hurting and hopeful—into this space?"

I said yes, trembling. I did not stand up and share all my business. My teams did not become my therapy group. But I also did not pretend everything in my life was tidy. I let people see that:

I asked for help.

I took time off for counseling.

I delegated more than my pride liked.

I said, *"I'm not at my best this week,"* instead of pushing through like a robot. Months later, one of the younger leaders I was mentoring said:

"Watching you lead while you were going through that gave me permission to believe that I won't be disqualified by my own hard seasons. I always thought I had to get over everything first."

That's when I realized: The very thing I thought disqualified me from leading was what God used to disciple someone else. **You don't lead after your wilderness. You often lead in it.** Unfinished leadership is not about showcasing your wounds. It's about refusing to fake a wholeness you don't yet have.

Letting People See Your Edges—Without Making Them Your Healer

There is a tension here. On one side: Over-sharing. Making your team carry your unresolved pain. Using your position to process inappropriately.

On the other: Under-sharing. Projecting invulnerability. Leaving people alone in their own struggles. Unfinished leaders learn a middle way: *appropriate vulnerability.* You let people see your edges without handing them the job of fixing you.

STORY: The Staff Retreat Where I Told the Truth (and Stopped Short)

At a staff retreat, I felt led to talk about burnout and limits. I could have kept it generic: *"Leaders need rest. Take care of yourselves."* Instead, I sensed it was time to go first. I said:

"In the last year, I realized I was pushing past my limits in ways that were not sustainable. I was saying yes too much, sleeping too little, and quietly resenting the very work I love. I've started seeing a counselor. I'm learning to say no more often. I'm still in process."

The room was very quiet. I did not: Go into graphic detail about my personal life. Cry in a way that turned the room into my support group. Ask them to fix or comfort me. I simply named that their leader was human, had gotten it wrong, and was now doing something about it. Afterward, one of my directors pulled me aside.

"I didn't know we were allowed to admit that," she said. "I've been struggling with the same thing but felt like I had to hide it because you seem to carry so much so well." We ended up revamping our entire approach to workload and sabbath rhythms over the next year. That wouldn't have happened if I'd kept performing. Appropriate vulnerability is not dumping. It is disclosure with purpose:

To normalize growth.

To remove shame.

To invite healthier patterns.

You are not asking your people to be your healers. You are modeling what it looks like to seek healing.

When Your Growth Threatens the System

Leading from an unfinished place means you are changing.

Not everyone will be excited about that. Some people are invested in the version of you that: Never said no. Always took the late-night call. Never pushed back. *Carried most of the weight.* When you start setting boundaries, resting, telling the truth more directly—some will feel betrayed. They will say: "You've changed.", "You used to be more available.", "You're not as spiritual as before.", "You've become selfish."

STORY: The Volunteer Leader Who Didn't Recognize Me Anymore

In one ministry context, I had been the "yes" person for years. If something needed to be done, people looked at me. I always found a way.

As I grew in unfinished leadership, I started protecting my sabbath and my family time more fiercely. One weekend, a leader called asking me to speak at a last-minute event. Old me would have rearranged everything. New me looked at the calendar and said, *"I can't this time. I have a commitment with my family."*

Silence.

Then: "Wow. Okay. I guess we'll find someone else."

Their tone stung.

A few weeks later, someone mentioned, "*They were saying you're not as 'sold out' as you used to be.*" My first reaction was anger. Then shame. Then, strangely, relief. Because here was the truth: I had changed.

I was no longer willing to sacrifice my whole self on the altar of being seen as "*sold out.*" Unfinished leadership sometimes means grieving:

The version of you that people were comfortable with.

The roles you can't keep playing.

The praise you used to get for over-giving.

You will have to decide:

Do I want to be admired for a version of me that is slowly dying—or do I want to be faithful to the me God is actually forming?

Some people will walk away.

Some will talk.

Some will quietly adjust.

The ones who are also ready to grow will be grateful. They will see your shift as permission to make their own.

Developing Leaders Who Are Not Your Clones

When you've been through fire, it can be tempting to train people to avoid your specific mistakes. However, it I important to note that the people you lead are not you. Their story is different. Their wiring is different. Their temptations are different. *You are not raising clones. You are raising leaders.*

STORY: The Young Woman Who Led Differently Than I Did

I mentored a young woman—let's call her Kemi—who had obvious leadership gifts. She was:

Bold. Innovative. Less conflictavoidant than I was at her age.

My unfinished self wanted to shape her into my image:

"Be more cautious here."

"Don't be so direct."

"People won't like that."

One day, after a meeting, she asked, "Can I be honest?", "Of course," I said, bracing myself. She continued:

"Sometimes it feels like you're trying to protect me from making any mistakes by making sure I never do anything you wouldn't do. But I'm not you. I want your wisdom, not your fear."

Her words landed like a holy slap. I realized I had been discipling her from my wounds instead of from my wisdom. I apologized.

"You're right," I said. "I want to share the lessons I've learned, but I also want to see who you are as a leader. You're going to do some things differently than I would. That's not wrong. It might even be better."

Over time, I shifted from: *"Here's what you must do,"* to *"Here's what I did, here's why, here's what I learned. Now, how does that land with you? What feels true for your situation?"*

She flourished. She made some mistakes I had warned her about. She also took risks I would have avoided and saw beautiful fruit. Leading from an unfinished place means:

You don't use your story as a cage.

You offer it as a map—with room for detours.

Letting People See You Be Led

One of the most powerful things an unfinished leader can do is be visibly led. Not just by God in private. **By mentors. By counselors. By peers. By the people you lead.**

STORY: The Day I Brought My Coach into the Room

At one point, I was working with a leadership coach on some blind spots. She was helping me see patterns in how I avoided certain kinds of conflict. I could have kept that support hidden. Instead, I invited her to facilitate part of a team retreat. I introduced her by saying:

"This is someone who has been helping me grow as a leader. She's pointed out some ways I avoid hard conversations. Today, she's going to help all of us look at our patterns. "My team looked…surprised. You could see the questions on their faces:

"The president has a coach?"

"She's openly saying she avoids things?"

After the session, one staff member came up to me and said: *"I've always assumed I had to figure leadership out alone. Seeing you bring someone in to help you makes me feel less ashamed of needing help myself."*

Another said: *"I thought if I admitted to needing development, it would mean I'm not leadership material. Now I see it's the opposite."*

When you let people see you being led, you:

Normalize growth at the top. Remove stigma from asking for help. Create permission for everyone to be in process.

You are not abdicating authority.

You are demonstrating how authority stays healthy.

What It Feels Like to Be Led by an Unfinished Leader

Think of someone you follow: A boss. A pastor. A professor. A parent. A community organizer. Ask yourself:

Do I feel like I have to be perfect around them?

What happens when I make a mistake—do I expect punishment or process?

Have I ever heard them say, "I'm sorry," or "I was wrong"?

Do I know anything about what they are learning right now?

When people describe being led by an unfinished leader, they often say things like:

"I feel like I can bring my whole self, not just my shiny parts."

"I'm not afraid to tell the truth about what's not working."

"I've seen them change based on feedback—it makes me more open to it too."

"They don't pretend to know everything, but they know how to figure things out."

They are not describing a perfect leader. They are describing a safe one.

PRACTICE: The "Here's What I'm Learning" Circle

Choose one circle where you have influence:

Your leadership team.

Your classroom.

Your ministry group.

Your family.

Once a month, set aside 10–15 minutes for a simple practice: Each person answers two questions: ***"Here's one thing I'm learning about myself as a leader right now." "Here's one way I hope to grow in the next month."***

You go first. Not with a rehearsed, impressive insight. With something real. For example:

"I'm learning that I still avoid giving clear feedback when I'm afraid of hurting feelings. This month, I want to practice having at least one honest, kind feedback conversation each week instead of letting things pile up."

Or

"I'm realizing how quickly I jump into fixing problems instead of asking questions. This month, I want to practice listening longer before I offer solutions."

Over time, this does three things:

It normalizes growth as a shared expectation, not a private shame.

It reminds people that everyone—including you—is a work in progress.

It creates a rhythm of reflection that keeps you from leading on autopilot.

This is not a gimmick. It is a culture-setting habit.

Your Unfinished Life Is Part of the Curriculum

When I look back at the leaders who marked me most deeply, I don't just remember: Their sermons. Their lectures. Their strategies.

I remember:

The way they apologized without self-destructing.

The way they cried and kept going.

The way they changed their mind when new truth came.

The way they took a sabbath seriously.

The way they treated people who could do nothing for them.

Their unfinishedness didn't diminish their impact. It deepened it. It made their teaching three-dimensional. Your life is sending messages all the time:

"You are allowed to be tired and still called."

"You are allowed to change and still be trustworthy."

"You are allowed to get it wrong and make it right."

"You are allowed to ask for help and still be a leader."

You don't have to manufacture those messages. You live them. Imperfectly. Repeatedly. Honestly.

You Are the Evidence That God Uses Unfinished People

One of the enemy's favorite strategies is to convince leaders: "You are the exception. God can use other broken people, but not you." "Your story is too messy.", "Your doubts are too big.", "Your past is too loud." Look at the story you've lived. Really look.

The girl who thought she was too much.

The divorced woman who thought she'd never be trusted again.

The firstborn who carried adult burdens as a child.

The Black woman who walked into rooms that were not built for her.

The single mom who studied after putting kids to bed.

And yet:

You have taught.

You have led.

You have founded.

You have mothered.

You have mentored.

You have kept showing up.

You are not the exception.

You are the evidence.

The evidence that God prefers unfinished clay to polished statues.

The evidence that leadership is not a reward for having no needs, but a stewardship given to those who will keep growing in the midst of their needs.

Leading others from an unfinished place is not plan B. It is the only plan any of us actually have. You will not wake up one day suddenly finished. You will wake up, again and again, with:

New awareness. New invitations to heal. New chances to model what real, human, courageous leadership looks like. And as you do, the people watching you—students, staff, children, congregants, neighbors—will quietly learn:

"Maybe I don't have to be finished to start. Maybe I can lead, build, love, and serve as I am, while I become."

That is the legacy of an unfinished leader. Not perfection.
Permission.

CHAPTER 11

Staying on the Journey: Growth Across a Lifetime

In every season, I have discovered new ways I am unfinished. At first, this frustrated me. Now, I see it differently.

I have been:

A firstborn child.

A choir member.

A divorced mother of two.

A professor.

A college president.

A Business founder.

A remarried wife and mother of six.

A conference host and leadership expert.

Growth Is Not a Straight Line

We like to imagine growth as a clean upward graph: Up, up, up., Better, better, better. My life has not looked like that. Maybe yours hasn't either. My growth has looked more like: Spirals. Loops. Two steps forward, one step back. Surprise detours. Lessons I thought I had already learned—coming back at a deeper level. This is not failure. This is how humans grow.

Seasons of Expansion and Seasons of Deepening

Some seasons of my life have been about expansion: New roles. platforms. New numbers. New visibility. Other seasons have been about deepening: Healing. Therapy or spiritual direction. Slowing down. Reevaluating. Letting go. Both matter. If you only expand without deepening, you become wide and shallow. If you only deepen without ever acting, you become thoughtful and stuck. An unfinished leader learns to ask:

"What season am I in right now—expanding, deepening, or both?"

Planning to Still Be Growing Decades from Now

I do not plan to "arrive" as a leader. I plan to:

Still be learning in my 60s, 70s, and beyond.

Still be listening to younger voices.

Still be updating my mindset.

Still be healing parts of my story I haven't touched yet.

Still be adjusting how I love my family, my community, and myself.

If you think this sounds tiring, let me say this: It is far more tiring to pretend you are finished than to keep growing. Growth requires humility, curiosity, and courage. Pretending requires constant performance.

I choose growth.

Reflection: Your Long View

Ask yourself:

When you imagine yourself 10–20 years from now, what kind of person and leader do you want to be on the inside?

What are 2–3 qualities you want to keep growing: courage, tenderness, wisdom, boundaries, joy, patience, etc.?

What might you need to start—or stop—doing now to move in that direction?

PRACTICE: Write a Letter from Your Future Self

Take 10–15 minutes and imagine your future self—older, wiser, still unfinished, but further along.

Write a short letter from that version of you to the you who is reading this book right now.

What do they say?

About what really mattered.

About what you can release.

About how much you've grown.

About how proud they are that you didn't give up.

Keep that letter somewhere you can read it again when you forget who you're becoming. Growth across a lifetime sounds poetic on paper. In real life, it feels like:

Losing things you thought you'd never lose.

Becoming someone you didn't plan to be.

Circling back to old pain with new eyes.

Having to forgive yourself for who you were at 25 when you're 45.

It is not clean. It is not linear. It is holy.

The Shock of Meeting Yourself Again… and Again

Every decade or so, life will introduce you to a new version of yourself. Sometimes gently. Sometimes with a crash. You will look back at an earlier season and think:

"How did I survive that?"

"Why did I tolerate that?"

"Who was I trying to impress?"

You will also look back and think: "I was braver than I knew.", "I did the best I could with what I had.", "I was already leading before I had language for it."

STORY: The Box of Old Journals

One afternoon, I opened a dusty box in the back of a closet. Inside were old journals—from my twenties, thirties, early forties. I sat on the floor and started reading. There was the young wife praying for a marriage that would eventually end. There was the single mom begging God to help her pay rent and tuition. There was the new professor terrified to stand in front of a class. There was the emerging leader writing, "God, I think You're calling me to more, but I'm scared."

I felt a mix of emotions:

Tenderness for that younger me.

Embarrassment at some of what I tolerated.

Grief for what she didn't yet know was coming.

Gratitude that she kept going anyway.

I noticed something else: The same themes kept showing up.

Wanting to please everyone.

Feeling like an imposter.

Carrying too much responsibility.

Longing to be seen and safe at the same time.

At first, I felt discouraged. *"Have I really not grown?"* I thought. *"I'm still wrestling with the same things."*

Then I noticed the difference in how I was writing about them. In the earliest entries, my questions were panicked, desperate:

"What's wrong with me?" "Why can't I get this right?"

In the later ones, the tone shifted: "I notice this old pattern again. What is it trying to show me?", "I set a boundary today and felt guilty—and free.", "I said no and survived their disappointment."

The content of my struggles was similar, but how I carried them had changed. That's what growth across a lifetime often looks like: Not the disappearance of old themes, and the deepening of your response to them.

When Old Lessons Come Back in a New Costume

You might think you've "dealt with" something—only to face it again later. You learned to set boundaries with your parents. Years later, you have to set them with your adult children. You worked through insecurity as a young professional. Years later, you battle it as a seasoned leader entering a new field. You learned to grieve a divorce. Years later, you have to grieve a different kind of loss: children leaving home, parents aging, a changing body.

It can feel like failure.

It's not.

STORY: The Second Round of Imposter Syndrome

After years as a professor and college president, I stepped into a new arena—hosting conferences, consulting, being called a "leadership expert." You would think, after all that experience, I'd be past imposter syndrome. Instead, it came back, wearing a new outfit. I stood backstage at my own conference, listening to the introduction: *"Dr. Laide Alexander, founder, president, leadership expert…"*

The audience applauded. Inside, I heard the familiar whisper:

"Who do you think you are?"

"You're not John Maxwell."

"What if they're disappointed?"

It felt like being 28 again, walking into my first classroom.

I was tempted to shame myself: "You should be over this by now." "After all these years, really?" But I had learned something new since then. Instead of treating it as proof I hadn't grown, I treated it as a spiral: *"I've been here before. I know what this is. I also know what to do."*

I took a deep breath and reminded myself: *"This fear is a sign that I'm in new territory again." "I'm not the same woman who heard these thoughts at 28. I have more tools now."* I walked on stage not as a finished expert, but as a woman in another round of the same classroom—with more history, more grace, more self-compassion. Growth is not that you never revisit old fears. Growth is measured by how quickly you recognize these seasons and how gently you respond to yourself when they arise.

Seasons You Don't Choose

Some seasons of growth are chosen:

You sign up for the course.

You hire the coach.

You start therapy.

You take the new role.

Other seasons are not. They arrive:

With a diagnosis.

With a betrayal.

With a death.

With a global crisis.

You would never have picked them. You wouldn't wish them on anyone. And yet, they permanently alter your inner landscape.

STORY: The Detour I Didn't Want

There was a year when life knocked the wind out of me. Multiple losses, close together. Personal. Relational. Vocational.

Personal. I went from: Speaking on stages. Building programs. Saying "yes" to opportunities. To: Canceling engagements. Sitting on my couch, staring at the wall. Waking up each day asking, "How do I keep going?" It did not feel like a "growth season." It felt like survival. I was angry. At the unfairness. At the timing. At God.

I told Him so.

Out loud.

More than once.

I thought my leadership journey had been derailed. Looking back, I see it differently. In that forced slowing down, truths surfaced that I had successfully outrun for years:

Old grief I had never fully faced.

Patterns of overresponsibility I had called "servanthood."

Deep exhaustion I had numbed with productivity.

I didn't become "better" in that season. I became more honest. And that honesty changed the kind of leader I am.

Less quick to give easy answers.

More willing to sit with people in their pain without trying to fix it.

Less impressed with my own accomplishments.

More aware of how fragile and precious life is.

You don't have to label your hardest seasons "good" to acknowledge that they grew you. You can say: *"I hate that this happened. I also see how I am different because it did."* Both can be true.

Growing Older Without Growing Hard

A quiet fear many leaders carry is: "What if I become bitter?" You've seen it: The older pastor who is cynical about every new idea. The seasoned executive who treats younger staff with contempt. The veteran teacher who has lost curiosity and compassion. They didn't set out to become that way. Life, disappointment, and unprocessed pain did their slow work. Unfinished leaders take this seriously. They plan not just for promotions and projects, but for their soul in their 60s, 70s, and beyond.

STORY: The Older Woman Who Showed Me What's Possible

At a conference, I met a woman in her late seventies. She had led for decades—in ministry, in education, in community work. Her eyes were bright., Her laughter was quick., Her presence was soft and strong at the same time.

We sat together at lunch, and I asked, "How have you stayed so open? So kind? A lot of people your age are...tired and bitter." She smiled.

"Oh, I've had my bitter seasons," she said. "I've buried people I loved. I've been betrayed. I've had doors slammed in my face. I've watched things I built crumble."

I asked, *"What made the difference?"* She thought for a moment. Then she said: *"I decided a long time ago that I would let loss make me softer, not harder. Every time something broke my heart, I asked God to keep it from turning to stone. I kept making friends with people younger than me, so I wouldn't get stuck in my own era. And I never stopped letting people challenge me—even when I didn't like it."*

She leaned in. *"The day I stop learning from people twenty, thirty, forty years younger than me, that's the day I stop leading, even if I still have a title."*

Her words lodged in my spirit. I thought: **"That's who I want to be.** "Not the older leader who sighs, "I've seen it all. Nothing impresses me.", but the one who can say, *"I'm still surprised. I'm still learning. I'm still letting God rearrange me."*

When Your Capacity Changes

Growth across a lifetime includes a humbling reality: Your capacity will change. Not just increase, but also decrease in certain ways. The energy you had at 30 is not the energy you have at 55. The way you led with little kids in the house is not how you'll lead as an empty nester. The risks you take at 25 will look different at 65.

This is not regression. It is stewardship.

STORY: The Day I Realized I Needed More Recovery Time

In my thirties, I could: Teach all day. Go to an evening meeting. Stay up late prepping. Wake up and do it again. In my forties and fifties, that rhythm started to cost me more. After a full day of leading and an evening event, I would wake up feeling like I'd been hit by a truck. At first, I shamed myself.

"You're getting weak."

"You should be able to do this."

"Other people your age are doing more."

Then I remembered: *I have lived a lot of life in these years. My body is not a machine. It is allowed to need more recovery now.*

I started planning:

Fewer back-to-back late nights.

More buffers after emotionally heavy days.

More honest conversations with my team about my energy.

One younger staff member joked, "So you're just going to slow down now?" I smiled. ***"No," I said. "I'm going to last."*** Adjusting your capacity is not giving up. It is choosing longevity over short-term impressiveness.

Letting Go Without Losing Yourself

As you age, you will have to let go of things: Roles you once loved. Platforms you built. Influence you carried in certain spaces. You might retire from a position. You might hand an organization to new leadership. You might step back from being "the one" and become "one of many." That transition can feel like death if your identity is wrapped around being needed.

STORY: The President Stepping Down

When I transitioned out of a presidential role, people asked: "Are you excited?" "What's next?" I felt...grief. I loved that work. I had poured years of my life into that institution. Stepping down felt like:

Leaving a child. Losing a name. Walking away from a piece of myself.

The unfinished part of me worried:

"Who am I if I'm not 'President Alexander'?"

"Will people still listen to me without the title?"

"Did I peak already?"

In the months that followed, something surprising happened. I discovered parts of myself that had been waiting quietly in the wings:

The writer.

The mentor.

The conference host.

The woman who could sit with a friend for hours without checking her phone.

I also discovered*: "My voice did not belong to that office. It belonged to me—and to God." The title had been an assignment, not my identity.* Letting it go made room for new assignments.

Not lesser. *Just different.*

Unfinished leaders learn to bless their past roles without clinging to them. They say: *"Thank you for who I became here. I release you. I am still becoming."*

Planning for Future You

We plan for retirement financially. We rarely plan for retirement emotionally and spiritually. What kind of older person are you becoming?

Not what will you do? Rather, who will you be?

Try this:

> **PRACTICE:** A Conversation with Future You

Picture yourself 20–30 years from now.

Not as a fantasy super-you. As a real, older, still unfinished you. Ask:

What is the look in their eyes? Soft? Hard? Tired? Alive?

How do they talk about people who hurt them? With bitterness? With boundaries and grace?

How do they talk about God? With distance? With intimacy? With curiosity?

Then imagine that future you sitting across from you now.

What might they say? Maybe:

"You can stop trying to impress people who won't even be in your life in ten years." Or:

"Take care of your body. You'll want to walk without pain when you're my age." Or:

"Love your people now. These are the years you'll look back on and miss." Or:

"Don't wait to get help. The sooner you face this, the more years you'll have on the other side of it."

Write it down.

That imagined conversation is not magic. But it often reveals what you already know in your spirit.

Giving Yourself Credit for How Far You've Come

Unfinished leaders are often better at seeing how far they still have to go than how far they've come. You remember:

The sharp words. The mistakes. The seasons you're not proud of.

You minimize: *The healing. The courage.*

The ways you're different now.

STORY: The Student Who Held Up a Mirror

At a student gala, a former student came up to me. She said: *"Dr. A, I don't know if you remember this, but there was a day in class when you stopped the lecture because you could tell we were overwhelmed. You sat on the edge of the desk and just...talked to us. You told us we weren't defined by our grades. That moment changed something for me. I stopped seeing myself as 'the dumb one' and started applying to things I never thought I could do."*

I had no memory of that specific day. For me, it was just...a Tuesday. For her, it was pivotal. On the drive home, I thought: "How many times have I dismissed my own growth because it didn't feel dramatic to me?" Consider the daily, quiet choices you make:

To listen instead of defend.

To rest instead of grind.

To apologize instead of justify.

To tell the truth instead of hide.

These are growth. You may not feel fireworks each time. But they are slowly, steadily, reshaping your life—and other people's. Take five minutes and list:

Three ways you handle conflict differently now than ten years ago.

Three boundaries you have now that you didn't then.

Three lies you no longer believe about yourself.

That is evidence. Not that you are finished. That you are on the way.

You Don't Graduate From Being "Unfinished"

There will be days, even in your later years, when you will think: "I should not still be struggling with this." "I thought I was past caring what people think." "I thought I'd have more faith by now." On those days, remember: *Peter walked with Jesus in the flesh, saw miracles, preached at Pentecost—and still later had to be corrected about his prejudice.* Paul, seasoned apostle, wrote, *"Not that I have already obtained all this, or have already arrived at my goal..."* Mature leaders in every field quietly confess: *"I'm still figuring this out."* You will not cross some invisible line where you stop being human. You will not wake up one day beyond the reach of old triggers. You will, however, accumulate:

More tools. More perspective. More grace for yourself and others.

And you will, if you let God and life have their way, grow softer and stronger at the same time.

Choosing Growth Again (and Again)

At the end of the day, "staying on the journey" is not one big decision. It is a thousand small ones:

Choosing to tell the truth in a meeting instead of staying silent.

Choosing to go back to therapy after a hard session instead of quitting.

Choosing to apologize when your pride wants to walk away.

Choosing to rest when your old self would have pushed through.

Choosing to try again after a failure instead of sitting down permanently.

You will not always choose well. Some days, you will regress. You will hear old words come out of your mouth and think, "Did I really just say that?" You will catch yourself wearing an old mask and think, "I thought I threw this away." In those moments, you have another choice: Shame yourself, declare all your growth "fake," and give up. Or say, "Ah. There you are again. I know this part of me. I know what to do now." That second choice is where lifetime growth lives.

Not in never falling, but in how you rise.

Again.

And again.

And again.

You do not have to be finished to keep going. You only have to be willing.

To stay curious.

To stay humble.

To stay open.

To stay on the journey.

Reflection and Practice Notes

You Are Allowed to Be Unfinished

You Are Allowed to Be Unfinished

If you've read this far, let me say something clearly: You are not behind. You are not disqualified. You are not the only one who feels this way. **You are an unfinished leader.** *So am I.*

What I Hope You've Heard

I hope you've heard, through my story and your own:

That your unfinished places are invitations, not indictments.

That your story—every chapter—has shaped your leadership, and you can face it with honesty.

That your masks (Achiever, Fixer, Rescuer, Saint) protected you once, but don't have to define you now.

That imposter feelings, burnout, conflict, and shame are part of the journey, not proof that you're failing.

That your inner life—mindset, will, emotions, story—is the most important "leadership development program" you will ever attend.

That you can lead powerfully from a place of honesty, humility, and growth.

This Is Not the End—It's a Turn in the Road

Closing this book is not the end of your journey. *It's a turn.* From here, you get to decide: Will you keep performing "finished"? Or Will you embrace being unfinished—and still called, still useful, still growing? You do not have to change everything overnight. You do not have to fix your whole inner life this week. But you can:

Tell one new truth.

Set one new boundary.

Rest one hour earlier.

Say one honest "I don't know."

Ask one brave question.

Share one piece of your story with someone safe.

Take one step toward the leader you are becoming.

A Final Blessing for Unfinished Leaders

From one unfinished leader to another, let me bless you:

May you have the courage to see yourself clearly—and still be kind.

May you have the strength to lay down what is not yours to carry.

May you have the humility to keep learning and the boldness to keep leading.

May your home, your work, your community, and your inner life become places where being unfinished is not a shame, but a shared reality.

And may you never forget: your becoming is a gift to the people you lead.

You are not a problem to be fixed.
You are a person in process.
An unfinished leader.
And that is exactly who the world needs.
One More Thing Before You Go

Before you close these pages and turn back to your emails and meetings and family and lists, I need to tell you one more thing: The world you are going back into is starving. Starving for leaders who are:

Honest, not polished.

Present, not performative.

Human, not heroic.

You may not feel like a worldchanger as you load the dishwasher, answer a student's question, sit in a budget meeting, care for an aging parent, or send one more latenight text to a hurting friend.

But that is exactly where this book was always headed:

Not to a stage.

To your real life.

To the next room you walk into after you put this down.

In that room, your unfinishedness will try to make you shrink:

"Don't speak up."

"Don't set that boundary."

"Don't tell the truth."

I am asking you to do the opposite. Let your unfinishedness become your way in, not your excuse out.

When you feel small, remember: you have already survived more than this moment is asking of you.

When you feel fake, remember: your willingness to keep growing is more honest than any performance of perfection.

When you feel tired, remember: resting is part of leadership, not a break from it.

Somewhere, someone is watching you right now the way you once watched someone else. They are asking, silently:

"Is it possible to lead and still be real?"

"Is it possible to have doubts and still be faithful?"

"Is it possible to make mistakes and still be trusted?"

You are their answer.

Not because you will get it all right. Because, when you don't, you will:

Tell the truth.

Make it right.

Get back up.

Keep becoming.

If there is anything I want lingering in your chest when you think of this book months from now, let it be this: You are allowed to bring your whole, unfinished self into the spaces you lead—and when you do, you do not lower the standard of leadership, you raise it. So go back to your ordinary, holy life: To your kitchen table and your conference room. To your classroom and your sanctuary. To your group chat and your board meeting. Go back with this quiet, defiant conviction:

"I will not wait to be finished to show up.
I will show up, and that is how I will be finished—slowly, honestly,
over a lifetime."

And when the old voices return and tell you you're too late, too broken, too much, or not enough, may another voice rise louder:

"I am not behind.

I am not disqualified.

I am not alone.

I am an unfinished leader—*and I am exactly on time.*"

Let that be the sentence that tugs at you when you are tempted to disappear.

Let that be the thought that will not leave you alone when you consider going back to pretending.

Let that be the truth that sends you into the next season of your life with a strange, stubborn hope:

You are still in progress. And your progress is the point.

Yesterday, I was unfinished.

Today, I am unfinished.

Tomorrow, I will probably still be unfinished.

But hear me clearly:

Unfinished does not mean unaccomplished.

Unfinished does not mean unsuccessful.

Unfinished does not mean unimpactful.

Unfinished does not mean unauthentic.

Unfinished does not mean unworthy of trust, influence, or calling.

It means just this:

I am still being formed.

I am still becoming.

I am still allowing God, truth, time, and community to shape me.

Simply—beautifully, relentlessly—unfinished.

And so are you.

Next Steps: How to Use This Book

Next Steps: How to Use This Book

You've finished reading *The Unfinished Leader.* Now what?

I didn't write this book just for inspiration. I wrote it for transformation—in you, in your family, in your team, in your organization, in your community.

This section is here to help you use the book:

- Personally

- In small groups

- With teams and organizations

- In workshops, classes, and conferences (including *Why Move My Cheese?*)

Use what fits your context. Adapt the rest freely.

1. Using This Book for Personal Growth

If you are reading this book on your own, here are a few simple ways to go deeper without overwhelming yourself.

A. One Chapter per Week

Instead of rushing, walk slowly:

- Choose one chapter per week.

- Read it once for understanding.

- Read the reflection questions and answer at least one in writing.

- Pick one practice from the end of the chapter and actually do it.

At the end of each week, ask yourself:

- What did I notice about myself?

- What surprised me?

- What felt uncomfortable (in a good way)?

- What do I want to carry into next week?

B. Start a Leadership Journal

You don't need a fancy notebook. Just a place to be honest.
Use these prompts regularly:

- "Today I felt most unfinished when..."

- "A mask I noticed myself wearing was..."

- "I said 'yes' to __________ but I wish I had said 'no' because..."

- ***"One thing I'm proud of in my leadership this week is..."***

- ***"One thing I want to grow in is..."***

This isn't about perfect journaling. It's about paying attention.

C. Choose a Theme for a Season

You don't have to work on everything at once. You could choose:

- 30 days on honesty (Imposter Syndrome and masks)

- 30 days on boundaries (over-responsibility and burnout)

- 30 days on courage (conflict, hard conversations, asking for help)

- 30 days on soul care (rest, prayer, reflection, play)

Revisit the chapters that match your theme and practice just one or two shifts consistently.

2. Using This Book in Small Groups

This book works beautifully in:

- Leadership small groups
- Bible studies / faith groups
- Book clubs
- Peer coaching circles
- Staff fellowship groups

Here's a simple structure.

A. Group Rhythm: 8–10 Sessions You can design an 8–10 week journey.
For example:

Week 1: I ntroduction + Chapter 1 (Myths of the Finished Leader)

Week 2: Chapter 2 (Inner Life)

Week 3: Chapter 3 (Our Stories)

Week 4: Chapter 4 (Masks: Achiever, Fixer, Rescuer, Saint)

Week 5: Chapter 5 (Teaching / Guiding While Unfinished)

Week 6: Chapter 6 (Imposter Syndrome)

Week 7: Chapter 7 (Burnout & Over-Responsibility)

Week 8: Chapter 8 (Conflict & Criticism)

Week 9: Chapter 9 (Soul Care)

Week 10: Chapters 10–11 + Conclusion (Leading Others &
Lifelong Growth)

You can shorten or extend this based on your time.

B. Sample Meeting Flow (60–90 minutes)
Check-In (10–15 min)

"Where did you feel most unfinished this week?"

"What's one win, one struggle?"

Read / Recap (10–15 min)

Either read key sections aloud or ask 1–2 people to briefly recap
the chapter in their own words.

Discussion (30–45 min)

Use 3–5 questions such as:

- What part of this chapter felt uncomfortably true for you?
- Which story resonated most with your own experience?
- What myth or mask did you recognize in yourself?
- How does this show up in your leadership at home? At work?
- What is one thing you want to try differently this week?

Practice / Commitment (5–10 min)

Ask each person to choose one practice from the chapter, or one small step of their own.

Have them say it out loud: "This week I will..."

Closing (5–10 min)

Optionally, a short prayer, moment of silence, or blessing.

Or a simple question: "What are you taking with you from today?"

C. Group Agreements

Because this book goes deep, set safety agreements:

- What's shared here stays here.
- We listen to understand, not to fix.
- We honor different journeys and cultures.
- We speak about ourselves, not for others.
- We are allowed to be unfinished in this group.

3. Using This Book with Teams and Organizations

If you lead a team, staff, department, or organization, this book can become a shared language for healthier culture.

A. Leadership Team Study

Start with your core leadership team:

Give everyone a copy.

Read one chapter every two weeks.

In meetings, use 20–30 minutes to discuss how the chapter applies to your context.

Questions to consider:

- Where is our team pretending to be "finished"?
- How do our structures encourage or punish honesty about being in process?
- Where are we over-responsible as leaders? Where are we rescuing instead of developing?
- How can we build rhythms of rest and reflection into our work?

B. Culture Conversations

Use key chapters (on masks, burnout, conflict, soul care) as culture conversation starters:

Host a brown-bag lunch or online session.

Read a short excerpt aloud.

Ask 2–3 powerful questions:

"What would it look like for us to normalize being unfinished here?"

"How do we currently handle mistakes?"

"What needs to change in our expectations so people can grow, not just perform?"

C. Integrate into Onboarding and Development

You can:

Make this book part of your leadership development track.

Assign specific chapters to new leaders and debrief one-on-one.

Use reflection questions as coaching prompts.

For example, in a one-on-one, you might ask:

Which mask do you wear most often in your leadership here?

Where do you feel most like an imposter in this role?

How can we support your growth in that area?

Use This Book in Workshops, Classes, and Conferences

If you teach, train, or run events (including the 'Why Move My Cheese' conference), this book can be a core resource.

A. Half-Day or Full-Day Workshop

You can design a workshop around 3–4 major themes:

Option 1: Core Unfinished Leader Intensive

- Session 1: The Myth of the Finished Leader (Ch. 1–2)
- Session 2: Story and Masks (Ch. 3–4)
- Session 3: Imposter, Burnout, and Conflict (Ch. 6–8)
- Session 4: Soul Care and Leading Others (Ch. 9–10)

Option 2: Focused Tracks

- Track A: Inner Work (Ch. 2–4, 9)
- Track B: Outer Work (Ch. 5–8, 10–11)

Use short teaching segments from the book, then move into:

- Guided reflections
- Pair or small-group discussions
- Role-plays for hard conversations
- Planning next steps

B. Course or Class

For a multi-week course (e.g., university, Bible school, leadership academy):

- Assign 1–2 chapters per week.
- Use the reflection questions as graded or ungraded journaling.
- Have students write a short paper or project on:
  - Their leadership story
  - Their masks
  - A growth plan for one unfinished area

C.   Conference Integration (e.g., 'Why Move My Cheese')

At your 'Why Move My Cheese' conference, you can:

- Give the book as a conference resource.

- Use selected chapters as the backbone of keynote talks or breakout sessions.

- Invite participants to identify:

  o   One myth they're leaving behind

  o   One new practice they're taking home

You can also create a reflection booklet (adapted from the chapter questions) for attendees to use during and after the event.

5. A Simple 7-Day Starter Journey

If someone wants to start small, here's a 7-day on-ramp:

- Day 1: Read Introduction and write: "Where do I feel most unfinished as a leader?"

- Day 2: Read Chapter 1 – Name one myth you've believed about leadership.

- Day 3: Read Chapter 2 – Do the 5-minute daily check-in.

- Day 4: Read Chapter 3 – Sketch your leadership story in seasons.

- Day 5: Read Chapter 4 – Identify your primary mask (Achiever, Fixer, Rescuer, Saint).

- Day 6: Read Chapter 7 or 9 – Choose one act of soul care or one boundary.

- Day 7: Read Chapter 10 or 11 – Write a note to your future self as an unfinished leader.

This gives people a taste of the journey and often draws them into a deeper read.

6. A Final Word as You Put This Book to Work

Everything in this "How to Use" section has one purpose: ***To help you take what you've read and turn it into how you live.*** You do not need to implement all of this. Choose:

One way to use it personally.

One way to use it with at least one other person.

One way to seed it into your team, class, or community if you lead others.

Remember:

You will not use this book perfectly.

You will not apply every idea.

You are allowed to experiment, adjust, and grow as you go.

You are an unfinished leader.

That doesn't disqualify you from using this book.

It qualifies you to use it honestly.

And that is where real transformation begins.

Notes

About the Author

D r. Laide Alexander has spent her life leading while unfinished. The firstborn in her family, she carried responsibility long before anyone called it "leadership." As a young woman, she led worship with shaky knees, discovering that saying "yes" while afraid is often how leadership begins.

For nine years, she raised her two children as a divorced mother—serving as mom and dad, protector and provider, teacher, preacher, nurse, and chauffeur. Those years of single parenthood formed a leader who understood sacrifice, resilience, and the quiet courage of showing up when no one sees your tears.

Academically, Dr. Alexander holds a first degree in Business Management, an MBA in Human Resources Management, and a doctoral degree in Educational and Leadership Management. She is currently completing a post-doctoral program in Applied Behavior Analysis (ABA), further deepening her understanding of human behavior and change. Her numerous certificates in leadership and project her lifelong commitment to growth and excellence.

Professionally, Dr. Alexander has served as a professor, shaping minds and hearts in the classroom, and as a college president, tasked with turning around underperforming departments and institutions.

She is the founder of Accexx Insight LLC, a consulting firm dedicated to helping leaders and organizations navigate change with clarity and courage, and the Founder and Chair of The Transformation Platform, a movement and space for leaders committed to deep, sustainable growth.

Today, Dr. Alexander is a leadership development expert, transformational coach, and the founder and host of the annual "Why Move My Cheese" Conference, where she equips leaders across sectors to embrace change, confront limiting myths, and grow from the inside out. She speaks at conferences, churches, universities, and organizations, bringing a rare blend of honesty, humor, academic depth, and practical wisdom.

At home, she is a remarried wife and mother of six, leading a beautifully complex blended family. Her greatest testing—and refining—as a leader still happens around the dinner table, not just on stages.

Across all these roles, one theme has remained:

She has never stopped being unfinished.

In *The Unfinished Leader,* Dr. Laide Alexander challenges the myth of the polished, perfect leader. She draws from her own story, her academic training in business, human resources, educational leadership, and behavior analysis, and the stories of countless leaders she has served. She invites readers to embrace growth over performance, courage over pretending, and soul health over burnout.

When she is not teaching, speaking, or writing, you can find her laughing with her family, mentoring emerging leaders, or quietly recharging with a good book—still growing, still listening, still becoming.

www.ingramcontent.com/pod-product-compliance
Lightning Source LLC
Chambersburg PA
CBHW020322180726
47991CB00018B/319